DIRTY NEWS

WHOSE $$$ PAYS FOR THE NEWS YOU TRUST?

by
PENNY FLETCHER

Table of Contents

Introduction
History Helps Us Understand Today's Headlines

Whose money is behind the publication you read, the radio station you listen to, or the television station you watch? Following the money is crucially important in learning about the people, corporations, and organizations that are changing the nation financially, environmentally, or treating certain people or groups differently than others.

Knowing who is behind your news reporting is especially important, and this book is written specifically to show you how to find out.

If you aren't sure of a source, follow the money. But we won't be pointing any fingers or giving lectures here. We will only have facts in this book unless specifically marked **EDITORIAL OPINION**. So, when I say, "follow the money," you will just see amounts and names. There will be no inference about whether these things are "good" or "bad," Red or Blue, or any other distinctions made by most mass media today. That, you see, is the deeper purpose of this book. To give you facts so you can make up your own minds about what is going on with the media and what happened that allowed it to be this way. But I have to tell you a little about myself in the first chapter, so you will understand what happened in a newsroom where I worked that made me realize just how different news had become since I started writing it.

Future chapters will include federal regulations, court cases, and reports that can be quickly checked on the Internet, most of which will be dated before 2016. The earlier dates were chosen deliberately so as not to add fuel to the fires currently burning, causing even more division between American citizens than there is now. And yes, there will be more first-hand accounts throughout other chapters of this book. But in Chapter One, I want to introduce myself because I'm writing this in a nonconfrontational, conversational tone and presenting facts that

show you, not "explain to you," what I've seen, studied, and followed these last thirty-eight years as a journalist. And oh boy, have things changed since CBS longtime anchorman Walter Cronkite was named "the most trusted man in America" in 1972. Today, just saying you're a journalist makes some call you a liar right to your face.

1

Who's Writing This & Why

"By skillful and sustained use of propaganda, one can make people see heaven as hell, or an extremely wretched life as paradise. Make the lie big, make it simple, keep saying it, and eventually, they will believe it."

Adolf Hitler

Adolf Hitler was an Austrian-born German politician who was the dictator of Germany from 1933 to 1945. He rose to power as the leader of the Nazi Party in 1933 and then assumed the title of Führer in 1934.

I deliberately used Hitler's quote at the top of this page to illustrate how powerful words can be. There will be many quotes from world-famous reporters, authors, and heads of corporate media throughout this book that amount to pretty much the same thing, but I doubt any can make "word usage" clearer than the sick feeling most of us get when hearing them come from Adolf Hitler.

Words are tricky because we see things based on our culture, past experiences, and belief systems.

For example, a hundred people witness an accident and give a hundred different accounts. Ask any investigator, law enforcement officer, insurance adjuster, or judge. And that's just for starters. Most of us encounter situations all the time where two or more people witness an event, and they all recall it differently.

Just how much does a viewpoint formed by tradition or culture influence the way we see the world? Or do observers see varying images of what's happening due to their particular brain wiring? That is a new theory being studied now at many forward-thinking institutes, including the National Institutes of Health in Bethesda, Maryland, and others.

Some things, however, are seen differently based solely on a person's identity. For instance: Is Benedict Arnold a hero or a traitor? What about Chief Sitting Bull and George Custer? Who's the hero there? Was Jefferson Davis a rabble-rouser and Abraham Lincoln a saint, or was it the other way around? Do we know? Do we *really know?* Or do we just know what we can see from our specific place in history, our family heritage, and the political viewpoints we've formed over time by what we have witnessed or heard?

You see, facts don't change. Only perception of them does. So, this book is dedicated to seeking out facts, but only by looking back at history can we truly understand how they relate to current events. Sometimes even the history books conflict as knowledge of new viewpoints unfolds. Seventy years ago, all pioneers taking over land in the American West were still portrayed as heroes for moving Indigenous Tribes off their land and farming it. Two hundred years ago, plantation owners were regarded highly for owning large numbers of slaves to increase productivity and the country's economy.

Thomas Jefferson, the principal framer of the Declaration of Independence and the third President of the United States, owned more than six hundred human beings during his lifetime. His well-used quotes about liberty are taught whenever people study the founding of the United States. Yet, he kept approximately four hundred slaves at Monticello over his lifetime. History books claim it took about a hundred-and-thirty at a time to run it, and the rest were kept on his other lands and properties. I doubt Jefferson's slaves (as well taken care of as they *probably* were) saw the word *liberty* the same way Jefferson did when he framed the Declaration of Independence. Don't you?

But this book isn't about slavery, or the killing of American Indians, or new scientific theories of brain activity during the observation of events. It's about what's happening in our world, especially here in the United States. It's about sorting through history and current events and digging for today's truth. Yes, truth is out there. But where?

As a journalist for almost forty years, I can honestly say I tried as hard as possible to stay away from using biased tips and sources. I've received more than twenty awards for hard news, features, editorials, and commentary. I'm telling you this so you can check me out as your source because much of the material included in this book will be about the need to check your source, and in the last chapters, we'll talk about exactly how to do it.

Checking your source is vitally important, especially now, because our country is so divided. Friends and family who once did everything together aren't even speaking. Groups turn into rioting mobs quickly, sometimes before anyone can tell what (or who) started it. Bias seems to be everywhere, and many see their long-time family, neighbors, and friends as only Red or Blue.

Checking your source is also important because today's newsrooms are driven by money, and news organizations without lots of it are fast disappearing. This book will explain how it felt to be part of the changes as buyout-after-buyout took away our freedom to see a completed news story the way we originally wrote it.

The people I've worked with over the years will *all* say I write the truth as I see it- every time— even if it comes to a face-off with the company brass and means my job. As an old-school journalist, I can look around and see drastic changes in the way national and international news are reported today. That means the closer a reporter (print or broadcast) is to the community they serve, the better the chance those reporters are writing the truth. If they live and work in their coverage area and interact with their readers during nonworking hours, they have to be more responsible for what they report. Think about that before you toss out the local "rag" that's thrown in your driveway or left free in stores or a newspaper rack.

The problem with this is that those local presses (and even some smaller broadcast stations) are restricted to posting only hyperlocal news. That means you will know the truth about when a pothole on your town's main street will be repaired, when a new development is going to be built in your community or a new business opens that you might want to visit. But that's all that hyperlocal news can do. It may be more accurate, but it doesn't reach outside your community like state, national, and international news.

One big problem with this is that national and international news are reported mainly by journalists who are now often regarded as celebrities and have jobs that pay a lot more money than the salary of any United States Senator or Congressperson. The days of the dedicated reporter and editor sitting up all night in a smoke-filled newsroom to get the truth out about something you missed that you need to know about have been replaced by "canned news" sent to scores of affiliates from a corporate office somewhere far away and supported by influential people, corporations, and PACs we never see and may not even know exist.

So, lesson number one in *following the money* is to ask if it makes sense that the person reporting what you're hearing, reading, or viewing would want to preserve the status quo, press for an agenda of change, or report things precisely as they happen. Sometimes we don't have to look very far to find out if they have a personal interest in what they're reporting, and sometimes it's hidden pretty deep. This relatively short book isn't for the faint-hearted or the politically correct. It's entirely too blunt for that. But it will be objective, without any slant. The goal here is to present the work of reporters and their first-hand experiences from the best sources that can be found, not those of friends and family or any company or lobbyist, and certainly not from the viewpoint of any government official or agency. Its purpose is to examine how the news came to be entertainment (and is often false; embellished, or presented just to get ratings) and what went on —and is going on now— that allows it to be that way.

There are legions of frightened and dissatisfied people out there from all walks of life, from out-of-work moms and dads facing foreclosure to small business owners going under because of monopolies and chain stores. They want to know what's really going on and who they can believe so they can decide the best way to go forward with their lives. It's crucial that the truth be told and that everyone knows where (and how) to find it. I realize some people have their minds made up and don't want to hear anything that conflicts with their point of view. I hope those people will also read this book, but even if they don't, those of us who learn how to find the truth will have a better idea of how to speak with those who don't.

The lack of straight, unadulterated news didn't start with the Coronavirus pandemic or the 2016 primary elections. It started long ago. I only know this because, throughout the eighties, nineties, and early 2000s, my job as a reporter took me from million-dollar mansions to homeless camps and everything in between, sometimes on the same day.

I'm old. I'm seventy-six. I remember reading about President Dwight D. Eisenhower in *My Weekly Reader* in elementary school and his plans for national highways called Interstates. At the time, I thought that was the best thing I had ever read. Instead of mostly dirt and gravel roads, our '88 ragtop Oldsmobile could visit other cities and states in a shorter time, which meant we might actually have enough time for real vacations once we got there.

Growing up, I was really impressed by President Eisenhower and his lofty goals and plans, and to think he had been a General in the "Big War" too! Such an inspirational figure for us, as kids, to look up to and want to emulate.

Then came the brilliant speeches by President John F. Kennedy about the Space Race and how Americans needed to "give their best to get the best."

"Ask not what your country can do for you, ask what you can do for your country," Kennedy said during the Cold War years when we, as school kids, were practicing air raid drills where we dived under our desks with our arms around our lowered heads. The Big War was over, but the Cold War with the USSR (Union of Soviet Socialist Republics: meaning Russia and its outlying Russian-run countries) had just begun.

My point in mentioning these two Presidents is that I was seventeen when I graduated high school in 1963, and as a young, open-minded student, I thought highly of both a Republican and a Democrat. I was not brought up to adhere to a single political belief but to have an open mind and judge every individual by their actions. Political parties never mattered to me, so when I attained voting age, I registered as an Independent and often split my ticket between candidates of different parties.

I later learned that many states didn't allow Independents to vote in primaries, so I had to study the candidates and decide which Party I would sign up with each time a voting year came around. Since I did that anyway, it seemed natural that once I became a reporter, part of my newsroom job almost immediately became studying candidates' positions and putting them in fourth-grade language.

After a while, I was given the job of untangling ballot amendments too. The reason: because even as far back as the early 1980s, sometimes checking "Yes" (to an amendment that could make or change a law) really meant "no" because it was written in language that would deliberately confuse voters. We'll talk about that more later, with easy-to-follow examples.

While still young and impressionable, I "assumed" (a word, which when broken down means, "makes an ass out of you and me:" A-SS-U-ME) that most people judged political candidates as individuals. I found this attitude quite different from what I saw while interviewing in the 1980s and 1990s as a reporter for *Sunbelt Newspapers* in Hillsborough County, Florida, twenty miles southeast of Tampa. I'll give one example that will explain the moment my eyes were opened to the most dangerous kind of partisanship.

One of my most memorable all-time quotes was given to me by a former President of the Sun City Center Republican Club, Donna Lewis (name changed). That year, that particular club was supposedly the largest Republican Club in the country. That made sense to me because it was headquartered in a large, upscale, politically active retirement community. Still, I checked and found it was indeed the largest Republican Club, which warranted a local news story, so I promptly began interviewing her.

When Donna finished explaining her club's goals and accomplishments, I asked her to sum up how she felt in a quote I could use under her photo with the story.

It didn't take her but a moment to answer with, "I would vote for a monkey to protect the party's seat."

Stunned but not letting it show on my face, I asked her if she was sure she wanted that to be her quote.

"Well, of course," she said. "That's exactly how I feel."

I thought long and hard about using that quote, but I had given her a chance to take it back, and she didn't. So, we ran it under her photo, with the news story about the club, and she didn't seem to be the least offended.

Almost immediately following that story, I wrote about the Sun City Center Democrat Club to balance things out. I don't remember the year, but the president's name was Walt Williamson.

I mentioned these stories for two reasons: One, because I deliberately wrote about the Democrat Club even though there had only been a "timely reason" to write about the Republican Club. I reported on the Democrat's goals and accomplishments closely following the Republican story because one group had gotten its goals and achievements in print. Therefore, so should the other. Why? Because that is *how reporters used to look at what we wrote.*

My second reason for bringing this up here is that Donna's quote was important to her. And, I knew instinctively it was vital to the story because in a Republic, we send representatives to Washington to represent us, and that should mean we send those we think will do what we want and vote for the things we would vote for if we went there ourselves.

The fact that the head of any organization would send anyone just to hold a party seat was shocking to me at the time. *This must go on in a lot of places, maybe even by all the political parties,* I thought. To me, that meant the public had a right to know so they could watch for it, because that is also how we used to look at what we wrote.

I was still green enough to wonder why people couldn't set their differences aside so they could work together to solve the country's problems. By the late-1980s, it was getting more evident there were certainly enough problems that needed solving. So, I tried to seek out features about good people helping missions, food banks, and other worthy causes. I covered schools, sporting events, and people with talents of all kinds.

Sadly, as the years passed, the disparity between people and neighborhoods became evident and impossible to ignore on my four-hundred-fifty-square-mile beat, which extended North-South from the Manatee County line to a town called Brandon (just southeast of Tampa) and West to East from Tampa Bay, inland through fields, cow pastures, orange groves, and miles of substandard farmworker housing. **Please notice I just used the word *substandard*. That is my Editorial Opinion based on the fact there was no running water or sometimes even no electricity in the dwellings they occupied. Yet, it is still commentary because it is based on my feelings. Without using that one word, a complete description of the housing would have kept the paragraph to fact. These attempts to make you see something in a particular way will become much easier to spot as we proceed through the chapters in this book.**

Besides transient farmworkers, more homeless poured into our area each winter to keep from freezing to death up North. The East Coast was more populated and patrolled then, so it was our area, between Tampa and Bradenton, the next largest town to the south, where many homeless came.

So, I covered Metropolitan Ministries in Tampa, the Good Samaritan Mission in Balm, the Beth-El Farmworker Ministry in Wimauma, and at least twenty area churches that had groups gathering blankets for the homeless, donating clothing and shoes, and holding food drives of all kinds. I wanted to use my work to help, and I could see many people doing good things who felt the same way.

This allowed me to have tea in china cups in million-dollar homes and coffee in what had once been a corn can while sitting on old tires in the woods listening to the stories of homeless families and military veterans trying to stay warm around a barrel fire.

People asked me why I wasn't afraid to go into places like that, but I knew it was part of the job when I took it. I often thought about the brave reporters who had filmed the march across the Selma Bridge with Dr. Martin Luther King and how those television reports had reached New Jersey where I grew up, never having personally witnessed that kind of bigotry.

I know that was exactly what made me want to get involved in news, although that didn't happen for many years after I left New Jersey. But those early television reports from the Civil Rights movement made me realize it was important for all people to know what was happening in the world if there was ever going to be any betterment or change.

I did want to make things better, as did the others I worked with back in the day. But after a couple of buyouts, I realized it was getting really hard to write about a need for betterment or change, or even about the people who were trying to accomplish it.

Sometime in the '90s, after what I think was our chain's second buyout, that time by *Media General Communications Corp. Inc.,* based in Virginia (since then dissolved when bought by an even larger group), it didn't matter what I wrote because that wasn't *exactly* what got printed. I'll give one example of that here, so what I just said will be easy to understand.

One evening in the mid- 1990s, I attended a Community Association meeting in Sun City Center where they were voting on a budget to upgrade their amenities and clubhouse. Most of the people at the meeting were interested and in approval of a plan presented by the Association Board. Still, every once and a while, someone had an objection to a particular item. Naturally, I recorded those things as well as the overwhelmingly good response the plan received from the majority.

Back in the newsroom, I wrote the story about how well the plan was received, and somewhere in the body of the copy noted the objections, citing the names of the people who had made them and why.

When the paper came out, the office was filled with angry residents. The phones were jammed with calls.

"What's wrong?" I asked Olga Bayliss, our morning receptionist. She showed me the paper that had just come out. My headline and first graph had been completely changed to read (something like— I mean, it has been more than 25 years— so I'm saying "something like") *Residents Object to Board's Plan.* The objections not only headlined, but the paragraph that contained them was now the lead. Instead of an accurate blow-by-blow story about the meeting that someone who missed it could read and feel like they'd been there, our front page had a story with my name on it that was nothing like what I had turned in. Oh, ninety-nine percent of the copy was mine. It was just the headline on top and the out-of-context lead that made the objections look like the most important thing that had occurred at the meeting.

That was the first time (of several) I had a face-off with my new supervisor, who had recently come with the ownership change.

Before that buyout, I had been promoted to Bureau Editor and by then supervised two local newspapers (and their small staff) and continued to write hard news, features, business stories, and editorials. I knew all the communities we covered, and the people who lived in them knew me.

I was horrified at what had been done to my story about the association's meeting and knew immediately I would no longer be trusted once word got around, and not just in Sun City Center. We also covered the nearby communities of Wimauma, Ruskin, Sun City (different from Sun City Center), Gibsonton, Balm, Apollo Beach, and Riverview. The eight communities were together referred to then as East Bay and were very inter-related. Now, that same area of Tampa Bay is called SouthShore.

I remember saying, "You changed the whole tone of my story!" I know I used the word "tone" because I'll never forget what my new supervisor said after that.

"What do you mean by tone? All that matters is what happened."

He didn't understand the word "tone." Or why the tone of a story mattered. That was the first time I was told, "Just remember what goes above the fold has to make people pick it up instead of another paper."

I don't remember the rest of the conversation, but I know what it came down to was *we had to give the advertisers a reason to buy ads. And to do that, we had to be able to say we had the largest local readership, no matter what it took.*

That was the first time the changes in newsroom behavior hit me personally. But later, as I studied and kept up with news trends, I could see it was happening on a much larger scale across the country.

The only other personal experience necessary to the context of this part of the book is one where a line was taken out of one of my hard news stories. Just one line that started with: "Wrong man shot by sheriff's deputy..."

This came about when I covered a shooting outside an office where migrants started the legalization process. I wasn't there when the shooting happened, but the man who was shot in the back and killed was the father of two children who attended Sunday School at my church. Because their mother knew and trusted me, she asked me to go to the local funeral home with her to prove her husband, who was a U.S. citizen, was shot in the back. He was apparently assisting a group of people preparing for citizenship, waiting outside for the office to open. I don't have all the details anymore and am not going to give all the ones I do remember, just enough to explain how this relates to what was happening in the media world at that time. And remember, I was writing for a local readership. This wasn't even a national story.

I didn't go to the funeral home. I believed her story. I knew her and her whole family, including their children and the man who was shot.

I also knew the heads of the local sheriff's offices and interviewed them.

The dead man had indeed been shot by a local sheriff's deputy, who was after someone else in the crowd who had committed a crime. I did the best job I could with the story, representing all sides, including the fact that the deputy stated he was aiming for someone else.

My story went in as written, with one line absent. "Wrong man shot in the back (including his name) in a raid to capture (name) outside (name of business) in the Thriftway Plaza on U.S. 41, in Ruskin, Florida."

The story had been manipulated to satisfy our new bosses, who did not want to get on the wrong side of the local sheriff's department.

I cried when I read what had been printed because I knew the widow had singled me out because she trusted me. I still remember her name and the names of her two children all these years later.

This is really all you need to know about me at this time unless you want to check me out as your source, which I have already said is *always* a good idea. You'll find my website and other online coordinates in the back of this book.

The following chapters will deal with the laws and court rulings that have changed, allowing for such drastic differences in what we see in the news today. But be of good cheer. There are still ways to find the truth, and in the last two chapters, I will lead you through them one by one.

2

The Gradual Demise of 'The Fairness Doctrine'

This is not to be confused with the 'Federal Equal Time Law,' which only applies to politicians and political candidates. We'll be taking that up in a separate chapter. This Doctrine applies only to legislation governing airwaves at the start of radio and television. This chapter is meant to explain why the rules in the Doctrine were confusing from the start, changed a little at a time, and eventually deemed unnecessary and eliminated. These changes are what legally allow the "slanted, biased, or one-sided news" we often see or hear today.

Now that we've talked about a few changes that affected me first-hand in the 1990s let's look at the intricate balancing act and the thin line between legislation intended to present a fair representation of all sides of issues and those protecting free speech and free press.

Anyone who starts falling asleep or losing interest while reading this chapter just skip it and go on to the next. It is the only chapter filled with court decisions, direct quotes from those decisions and the Justices who made them, and Congressional Acts. I included it for those who want to follow what happened that has allowed much of the media to become what it is today: often one-sided, and sometimes nothing more than advertising, opinion, or entertainment disguised as news.

It took a long road to get to this point, and that road was filled with the court decisions and Congressional Acts found in this chapter. I simply want to give those who wish to follow the line of thinking and reasoning behind those decisions the chance to do so. For those who want to look closer, I offer links to many of the important decisions to which I refer.

The rest of you just skip to the next chapter. However, I do caution that not knowing the details behind the many changes that took place during the last hundred years and why they occurred will impede your understanding of today's media.

And so, the technical part of our journey begins:

* * *

We could go back to legislation concerning all types of communication that existed as far back as 1889, but that isn't necessary since The Communications Act of 1934 tried to incorporate everything that had ever been written concerning any type of *communications,* making that a much easier (and later) date to start.

The 1934 legislation was massive. It attempted to govern all types of public communication, from railroads to broadcasting. Until then, broadcasting had been treated separately because airwaves are different from other public "carriers" (like railroads).

The same 1934 legislation (The Communications Act established by Congress) also instituted the Federal Communications Commission, which still exists today.

From its beginning, the FCC was given the job of overseeing radio and later (in the 1950s) television. Still, it was not separated from other types of communication, which resulted in many court cases because of the language used.

It was confusing because the 1934 Act kept some portions designed for transportation services— primarily railroads— written in 1889 and also kept some of the 1910 legislation that extended its authority to interstate commerce of "all types of communications."

Wow! Physical communications and airwaves communications in the same act. Yes, that is fact. **But "Wow" is an Editorial Opinion, which in this book will always be marked as such in bold. Showing how to spot even the most innocent of Editorial Opinions is one**

of the two primary purposes of this book. How news came to be slanted and often wholly untrue is its second purpose.

The newly-formed Federal Communications Commission supplanted a portion of the Radio Act legislation. Congress instructed the FCC when it was created to use a "Fairness Doctrine" to ensure that all sides of issues were reported. The intention was that holders of *all* broadcast licenses present *all* news, especially of controversial or political significance, and in fact, any matter of public importance, in a fair and balanced manner. Portions of its exact wording on this were, "All news...always honest, equitable, and balanced."

The doctrine had two essential elements.

1) It required broadcasters to devote some of their time to giving *all* news of controversial public interest

2) And to "air any and all contrasting views on the matter."

Stations were allowed an extensive range of ways they could provide these contrasting views. They could use news segments, public affairs shows, or editorial opinions. The doctrine never required equal time for each view but did require *any and all views* on an issue to be presented. The doctrine cited the reasoning behind this as "to be sure listeners were exposed to a range of viewpoints so each person could make up his or her own mind on issues." In the 1950s, with the advance of television into most US homes, the FCC extended The Fairness Doctrine to TV as well.

Besides everything already mentioned, the same 1934 Act also stated that "common carriers" like railroads, public utilities, and broadcasting "should be available to everyone at a reasonable price *and were not the originators of messages or content.*"

Editorial comment: the wording I italicized in the sentence above appears as if they were treating what was said on radio as the relaying of messages, not anything that had originality. Yet *editorial*

opinion was one of the allowable counter-balances they wrote into the FCC rules. The Act seemed to contradict itself from the beginning, leaving it open to many challenges, as you will see later in this chapter.

Back to Direct Quotes: "The (same) 1934 Communications Act also covered telephone messages and recognized AT&T as a monopoly." The monopoly was permitted to exist until broken up by Congress in 1984 because at the time the 1934 Act was written, it said, "AT&T can be a monopoly because the American Telephone and Telegraph was established in 1913 and was approved by Congress to provide the necessary efficiency for both national and universal phone service."

The same piece of 1934 legislation also:

1) Granted licensees of radio frequencies sole control over their frequency

2) Required broadcasters to develop public interest programming

3) Made no provision for a public broadcasting service, rejecting a proposal to allocate twenty-five percent of the broadcast spectrum for nonprofit and educational stations

4) Required broadcasters to provide the platform for discussing controversial issues

5) Used wording to show that Congress recognized airwaves as public property, not to be owned; noting public necessity and convenience

It didn't take long before claims were made that portions of this doctrine interfered with First Amendment rights, which fall under Congress and/or the courts, so claims of First Amendment infringement (connected to the Fairness Doctrine) could not be settled solely by the FCC.

So, before even talking about news content— and why it isn't the same as it used to be, we must understand how the rules written in the 1934 Act became obsolete with progress and why they were gradually removed.

An excellent example of how these rules were first tested is shown in the 1969 case of *Red Lion Broadcasting Company v The FCC* in the United States Supreme Court. In this case, Justice Byron White wrote the majority opinion that upheld the constitutionality of The FCC's Fairness Doctrine by saying, "broadcasters must offer time to reply to someone who had been attacked or criticized on the air." He added that "the airwaves are a public good that the government *can* regulate, even if it means the activities of the broadcast press are restricted."

The case began over a book written by Fred Cook criticizing the 1964 Presidential candidate Barry Goldwater, titled *Barry Goldwater, Extremist on the Right*. A radio station owned by *Red Lion Broadcasting Company* in Red Lion, Pennsylvania, ran a fifteen-minute broadcast of the Rev. Billy James Hargis criticizing Cook, saying he had been fired from the *New York World-Telegram* newspaper for false charges against a New York City official. It also stated that Cook, while writing for *The Nation*[1] (which Hargis *said on air* had "championed many communist causes"), had also accused him of "attacking the Federal Bureau of Investigation director, J. Edgar Hoover, and the Central Intelligence Agency on the air."

When Cook heard about the broadcast, he was livid and demanded free reply time to address the attack. The station refused him, but the FCC declared that the station must allow Cook to reply to allegations against him *"because it fell under the Fairness Doctrine."*

The station did not comply and took it to the courts, but the D.C. Circuit of the Court of Appeals upheld the FCC's decision. The case

---

1.   *https://www.britannica.com/topic/The-Nation-American-journal*

eventually ended up in the Supreme Court, which had to decide if the FCC had the authority to regulate the electronic media under The Fairness Doctrine, or if something like this instead fell under the First Amendment right of free speech, which would mean this type of thing didn't automatically get rebuttal time.

Once it was decided that it fell under the Fairness Doctrine, the Court added, "that it was "**also** consistent with the First Amendment goal of producing an informed public, capable of conducting its own affairs, which would allow persons who were attacked on a station to respond publicly on that same station."

"The airwaves are a public good the government can regulate," the Court opinion continued. **Editorial Opinion: Here, the Court seems to be trying to balance The Fairness Doctrine's right of rebuttal with the station's right to give a citizen free speech (without reprisal). But who in 1934 would have dreamed that Congress and the FCC would have any reason to battle over free speech vs. the responsibility to air valid content thirty years later? There were just twenty-three radio stations in the whole country when the Communications Act was written. Although television was officially invented in 1927, it was not common in US homes until the 1950s.**

Here are a couple more court cases to show how the courts continued to work with The Fairness Doctrine vs. First Amendment rights. Later we'll see how this comes into play in today's news programs even though the Fairness Doctrine no longer exists.

1) Justice White also wrote the Majority Decision in *Branzburg v Hayes* in 1972. That decision refused constitutional protection to journalists who claimed they should "have the privilege (notice the word *right* is not used here, but *privilege)* not to divulge sources to a grand jury. Justice White said he did not believe that "the absence of

this journalistic privilege would hamstring press operations," and stated the invention of *a new constitutional right* was not needed. The word (journalistic) *privilege* vs. the word *right* has not come into play in any court decision I could find recorded. This is what I found while researching cases: "The First Amendment privilege afforded to reporters is a qualified privilege; it is not absolute. The statutory privilege is limited to information obtained within the scope of the reporter's professional activities." To read more about this, click https://www.rcfp.org/privilege-sections/b-absolute-or-qualified-privilege/

2) Justice White further decided against journalistic privilege in 1978 with a majority opinion in *Zurcher v Stanford*. He wrote, "freedom of the press does not prohibit the government from executing searches of newsrooms per specific warrants."

**Many other rulings during his years on the Court can be found online that show how Justice White tried to balance First Amendment rights with government agencies as well as keeping a free media, and how members of the press felt about his rulings.

3) Another Supreme Court case that still influences us in politics today is the Court's 1973 ruling in *United States Civil Service Commission v National Association of Letter Carriers*. Yes, I said Letter Carriers. In this case, Justice White's Majority Opinion upheld the constitutionality of the Hatch Act, which prohibits government officials from forcing staff to engage in political activities on their superiors' behalf, and also further restricts "political speech activities of government employees."

By the mid-1960s, the way the issues were presented started to show up differently.

By then, the Supreme Court had said, "Airwaves are a scarce resource, and the spectrum will soon be overcrowded if everyone who wishes to have a broadcast station is permitted to have one." The wording of the Court adds, "The scarcity of stations creates the danger that some points of view may never be aired."

Clearly, this wording shows they were beginning to fear what would happen to the original Congressional principles of "airing all sides of issues" and "giving the public all the news so they could make free and informed decisions" if there was an onslaught of new stations, which is precisely what happened.

By the 1980s, scarcity was becoming a non-issue because of cable television expansion, so the Supreme Court then ruled that "It is the right of viewers and listeners, not the right of broadcasters, that is paramount..." And added: "The purpose of the First Amendment is to preserve an *uninhibited marketplace of ideas* in which truth will ultimately prevail, rather than to countenance monopolization of that market, to make sure there were enough broadcast licensees that all sides of issues be covered."

The treatment of print media did not follow the same rules. I am saying that as fact, not opinion, because I looked up some cases and chose the one mentioned next as an easy example to follow.

A different approach toward print media began as early as 1974 with the case of *The Miami Herald Publishing Co. v Tornillo,* when Chief Justice Warren wrote for a unanimous Court, "The government-enforced right of access inescapably dampens the vigor and limits the variety of public debate." The Supreme Court specified that decision, in this case, differed from *Red Lion* case because it "applied to a newspaper, which, unlike a broadcaster, is unlicensed and *can theoretically face an unlimited number of competitors.*"

Broadcasting rules did not follow the same principle.

In 1984, the Supreme Court ruled that Congress could not forbid editorials by non-profit broadcast stations that receive grants from the *Corporation for Public Broadcasting.* That case was called *FCC v the League of Women Voters of California.* The Court's five-to-four majority decision by Justice William Brennan Jr. stated that "while many say that the expanding sources of communication have made the Fairness Doctrine's limits unnecessary, we are not prepared to reconsider our longstanding approach without some signal from Congress or the FCC that technological developments have advanced so far that some revision of the system of broadcast regulation may be required."

After noting that the FCC was considering repealing the Fairness Doctrine rules on editorials and personal attacks out of fear that those rules might be "chilling speech," the Court added: "Of course, the Commission (FCC) may, in the exercise of its discretion, decide to modify or abandon these rules, and we express no view on the legality of either course. As we recognized in *Red Lion,* however, were it to be shown by the Commission that the Fairness Doctrine has reduced, rather than encouraged speech, we would then be forced to reconsider the constitutional basis of our decision in that case."

Here, the Supreme Court had to decide whether this was a case about First Amendment Rights, which Congress considers, or instead, an FCC matter, which would overturn the earlier decision by Justice White in *Red Lion in 1969,* that stated: "the airwaves are a public good that the government can regulate, even if it means the activities of the broadcast press are restricted." AND that it was "also consistent with the First Amendment goal of producing an informed public, capable of conducting its own affairs, which would allow persons who were attacked on a station to respond publicly on that same station." (Essentially, in that decision, the Court stated that the law accomplished *both* First Amendment Rights *and* that airwaves were a public 'good,' which meant the government, or FCC, could regulate them.)

EDITORIAL OPINION: This last statement, which tried to satisfy two separate requirements simultaneously, left the decision open to many future attacks. But hindsight is usually 20/20. The vast array of frequencies, radio and television, and now the Internet, could not possibly have been imagined in 1934 when the Act was written.

By 1985, under FCC Chairman Mark Fowler, a communications attorney, the FCC released its report on *General Fairness Doctrine Obligations* stating that the doctrine "hurt the public interest and violated free speech guaranteed under the First Amendment."

However, it is recorded (word for word)- that "the Commission could not come to a determination as to whether Congress had enacted the Doctrine in 1934 as part of the Federal Communications Act, or if the FCC had created the Doctrine *after* Congress had created the FCC." *That statement is perhaps the most important in this chapter because of what it produced next.*

**After moving through several investigations by Congress and the FCC, and many more references and cases that can be looked up online under the history of the Fairness Doctrine, the 99th Congress examined alternatives to the Fairness Doctrine. In 1986, it asked the FCC to submit a report (to Congress) on the effectiveness of the doctrine in light of new technology.

In 1987, in *Meredith Corporation v. FCC,* the case was returned to the FCC with a directive to consider whether the doctrine had been "self-generated pursuant to its general congressional authorization or specifically mandated by Congress." In simple language, the Court asked if Congress or the FCC (after being established by Congress) created the Fairness Doctrine?

Editorial Comment: It sounds like the records of the 1934 legislation were either lost, unreadable, or just ignored at this juncture, and due to their complexity, the Supreme Court sent the decision back to the FCC and washed its hands of it.

While pursuing this case, the FCC invited the public to comment on alternative means for administrating and enforcing rules then covered by the Fairness Doctrine. In the 1987 report, the alternatives—including abandoning the case-by-case enforcement approach, replacing the doctrine with open access time for all members of the public, doing away with the personal attack rule, and eliminating certain other aspects of the doctrine—were all rejected by the FCC.

Then, later that year, the FCC abolished the doctrine in the *Syracuse Peace Council* decision, which was upheld by a panel of the Appeals Court for the D.C. Circuit in February 1989. However, the Court stated in its decision that "the Justices made that determination without reaching the Constitutional issue involved."

Editorial Opinion: It seems this Court skirted the whole purpose of why the case had been brought to it. If its purpose was not to resolve a Constitutional issue, the FCC could have decided it without ever involving the Court.

Inserted into the *Syracuse Peace Council* decision was the following wording that the FCC requested: "Because of the many media voices in the marketplace, the doctrine be deemed unconstitutional, as the intrusion by government into the content of programming occasioned by the enforcement of the Fairness Doctrine restricts the journalistic freedom of broadcasters and actually *inhibits* the presentation of controversial issues of public importance to the detriment of the public and the degradation of the editorial prerogative of broadcast journalists."

The ruling also includes the sentence, "We seek to extend to the electronic press the same First Amendment guarantees that the print media have enjoyed since our country's inception." This means the regulations no longer applied because new technology, like newsprint, had so many competitors that to regulate it with the Fairness Doctrine would be restricting Free Speech like Congress had feared years before when it stated, "such regulation would *chill free speech.*" Remember that phrase from a few pages back?

Then, in 1996, The FCC overhauled its rules completely for the first time since 1934. To make a very long story short, it said, "The goal of its new *law* was to let anyone enter any communications business and to let any communications business compete in any market against any other." (Now the FCC is calling its rules *law*. Before this, FCC rulings were considered "rules.")

In 2011, The Fairness Doctrine was removed from the Federal Register. However, there have been recent attempts to reinstate the portions of The Fairness Doctrine that still make sense in today's world or write a new doctrine. We'll discuss these attempts in a later chapter when we talk about how media affects politics.

Editorial Comment & Opinion based on known facts:

Doing away with The Fairness Doctrine, followed by the 1996 FCC decision, opened the "Wild West" of slanted news. Broadcast and print media had been pushing the envelope with every challenge since the 1980s, and things began to radically change inside newsrooms because of it. Today there are many views in both print and broadcast, but many only present one side of an issue. People often tend to read or listen only to views that match their own, or of which they approve, therefore only getting one side of multi-faceted stories. It is easy to see that without *The Fairness Doctrine,* news is not always what it seems. Unfortunately, those who reached an age to follow the news since the doctrine's demise have never known anything else, and many who do know are using this new "Wild West" to filter out everything except their own agenda. Some lawmakers and activist groups are trying to fix this problem now, but the two major arguments are still the same. Stating that "all views must be presented on issues" with media being practically everywhere— especially on the Internet— seems

impossible to regulate; AND "could easily still infringe upon the First Amendment right to free speech and free press."

Should the Internet be regulated as broadcasting? Should it be regulated at all? Or is it already being controlled by the owners of its largest corporations? Keep reading, and we shall see.

3

Who Controls What We See & Hear?

"Our job is to give people not what they want, but what we decide they ought to have."

Richard Salant, (April 14, 1914 - February 16, 1993)

CBS Executive from 1952 and President of the CBS News division from 1961-1964 and 1966-79. Also, the author of the book "The Battle for the Soul of Broadcast News."

Known by the journalists of his time as the patron saint of television news, the late Richard Salant worked with *CBS News* through the 1960s and 1970s. He hired the most well-known and trusted news anchors of his day, including Mike Wallace, Dan Rather, Diane Sawyer, and Roger Mudd. Under his leadership, these journalists confronted significant issues, including President Richard Nixon's resignation in 1974 following the Watergate scandal. For those who do not know, in 1972, Nixon, a Republican, had ordered a break-in at the Democratic National Committee headquarters. A complete history of this event is recorded at HISTORY ONLINE: https://www.history.com/topics/1970s/watergate for those who care to read it.

During his tenure, Salant and his crew also covered the Vietnam War, the Civil Rights Movement, the shooting deaths of President John F. Kennedy in 1964, and in the spring and summer of 1968, the shootings of U.S. Attorney General Robert F. Kennedy and Civil Rights leader, Dr. Martin Luther King.

History credits Salant with launching the first thirty-minute *Evening News, CBS Morning News,* and the long-running, in-depth news show, which is still in progress, *60 Minutes.*

The quote at the top of this chapter comes directly from Salant and can easily be found just about anywhere his name is mentioned on the

Internet, and he was not the only news director to feel this way. That's because following the 1996 rewriting of FCC rules, large media got an even more significant boost in 2003 when the FCC voted to raise the number of media outlets a company could own in any geographical area.

People who were not involved in the buyouts may not see this as a big deal. I mean, don't corporations often own many stores or outlets in the same towns? But as I can show in one simple example, when it applies to media, that is far from the same thing.

When *Media General Communications Corp. Inc.,* headquartered in Virginia, took over all twelve local *Sunbelt Newspapers* in Hillsborough County, Florida, where I worked, it also bought Pasco County's affiliated twelve-paper chain *Suncoast Newspapers.* Then it bought out both *The Tampa Tribune,* one of Tampa Bay's only two daily newspapers, and *WFLA Channel 8* television in Tampa. At that point, it owned every news media in the large Tampa Bay area except a few small, hyperlocal newspapers and one daily paper, *The St. Petersburg Times.*

This was going on all over the country, and here's why.

Before the 2003 change, companies could only own enough broadcast stations to reach thirty-five percent of the population in any geographical area anywhere in the nation. But the new rule allowed this to rise to forty-five percent. That doesn't sound like much of a rise until you hear real numbers in the millions and then realize that forty-five percent is nearly half of every number of readers and viewers for miles.

Think about it: if you now own almost half the broadcast stations in a large geographical area and shut down almost all the print publications there, whose voice is going to be the only one people hear?

So, who does control what we see and hear?

Those who fund the media in large geographical areas control the content.

It isn't editorial opinion to say these "deep pockets" (which we will examine later) cherry-pick what will be broadcast in specific demographics because we will deal with that with facts in future chapters of this book.

Meanwhile, we will just discuss some of the larger buyouts that took place almost immediately after the 2003 regulation changes.

For example, within five years, ABC began a quest to take over its forty-five percent of media in many areas across the nation. That meant that all of them began resembling WABC in New York City, which then sent a lot of its national and international news to its affiliates across the country on a "must-run" status. Sometimes, even pre-written headlines and lead graphs were sent to make things easier for the affiliate anchors to convey the story in the context it was written to convey by the heads of its owner corporation.

Editorial Opinion: Humm... deciding on the headlines and lead graphs of stories. Close to what happened to me in Chapter 1, ya' think? This is why I cited a few first-hand examples earlier in this book. Some others I mentioned will make more sense later.

Even more rule changes took place in 2003.

One example is that a company was restricted to owning only two television stations in a big city in the past. After some FCC rule changes, companies could own three television stations in the same city. The old rules had also prohibited the same company from owning a newspaper and broadcast station in the same market, but the new rule also removed this prohibition.

Checking Congressional records shows most Republicans in power in 2003 supported the loosening of the FCC rules in the name of helping business, which they said would, in turn, would help the general economy. Most Democrats, however, wanted to stay with the rules created between 1941 and 1975, saying they promoted diverse opinions and encouraged competition.

When learning to recognize Slanted News or Editorial Opinion, know that if both sides of a two-sided idea are presented equally, like in the graph above that gave both the Republican and Democrat positions without stating one is better or worse than the other, it is NOT opinion. But whether it is a fact *must still be proven,* as we shall see in future chapters.

State regulators are allowed by law to recommend that the FCC prohibit mergers in smaller markets in which one company might attempt to buy up and control all the media in that market. But what constitutes a smaller market is open to interpretation and therefore open to abuse.

For example: Except for a few hyperlocal print and broadcast stations belonging to small communities within larger towns in the Tampa Bay area, the rest were all bought out by *Media General Communications Corp. Inc.,*as pointed out earlier— and then on January 11, 2017, the FCC approved the sale of *Media General* to *Nexstar Broadcasting Group* for $4.6 billion. Shortly after that, *Media General* was dissolved, and all twenty-four local print papers and *The Tampa Tribune* (daily) were shut down. At the same time, *Nexstar* began to operate *WFLA Ch 8,* so it became the *only broadcast source of local and national news coming directly out of Tampa.* There were other stations in nearby towns, some city and state government channels, and a PBS station nearby, but WFLA was the only national and international broadcast news source in the city.

You can check out Nexstar's political affiliations at https://www.opensecrets.org/political-action-committees-pacs/nexstar-media-group/C00567388/summary/2020 just in case you want to know more about what you've heard on a Nexstar station before you vote in the next election. As of January 2022, Nexstar owned 197 media outlets in the United States.

Almost immediately, *The St. Petersburg Times* changed its name to *The Tampa Bay Times,* signifying that there was still one daily newspaper based in the area covering both international and local news using local reporters. Even though most people living in the area didn't realize what had happened, they started talking about regretting the loss of their town's hyperlocal newspapers such as the Sunbelt and Suncoast chains, which had operated twenty-four papers concentrating on specific communities for years.

The former *St. Petersburg Times*(now *The Tampa Bay Times)* has won twelve Pulitzer Prizes since 1964 and has been on the U.S. top ten list of the best newspapers in the United States for years, and seems to have managed to keep fair news reporting because of its unique corporate structure. I'll explain that structure now so this won't look like an editorial comment.

The Tampa Bay Times is a for-profit news organization owned by the nonprofit Poynter Institute, which has been the preeminent journalism training organization in the nation since its inception in May 1975. The paper's publisher, *The Times Publishing Company,* also publishes the business magazine *Florida Trend* and the weekly newspaper, *TBT (Tampa Bay Times).*

But even those living in the area (let alone nationally) often do not realize this is what happened. They just know the *St. Petersburg Times* and *The Tampa Tribune* are no longer here, do not know the connection of the *Tampa Bay Times* to the Poynter Institute, or that Poynter also runs PolitiFact.

PolitiFact has always been known as a nonpartisan fact-checking website to sort out the truth in American politics. PolitiFact was created by the *St. Petersburg Times* in2007. The Poynter Institute acquired PolitiFact in 2018, which I have already said is a nonprofit school for journalists operated using the code of *The Society of Professional Journalists.*

However, in April 2019, Charles Koch, the Libertarian candidate for Vice President in 1980, joined his Foundation to this world-renowned organization by partnering in a Media & Journalism

Fellowship. Because the Koch Brothers' role in financing politics is an internationally-known fact, I have mentioned it here so Poynter and PolitiFact can be checked from time to time to ensure they are still on the list of the best reliable news sources we can use.

As of November 2021, as this book is being written, reporters I know and worked with who now work at *The Tampa Bay Times* say they write "straight news" just like they always did, even though they were unaware of Mr. Koch's partnership with their employer.

Editorial Comment: Just in case anyone thinks I am somehow affiliated with *Tampa Bay Times*, *The Poynter Institute*, or *PolitiFact*, I want to make two statements. 1) While working with *Sunbelt Newspapers* and *The Tampa Tribune*, I was fortunate enough to be sent to Poynter on two occasions for management training before it was associated with any outside partnerships. 2) Several good reporters I worked (and some I trained) at Media General News now work at the *Tampa Bay Times* and report facts as we did before, impartially. I only pointed out the 2019 connection to Charles Koch to make readers aware of the 2019 change as something they can look at in the future if they see a difference in reporting at a future time.

Before closing this chapter, I want to give one example I think everyone should hear. I must refuse to give my source because it was a high-ranking military official stationed at the United States Central Command Headquarters (while the US was in the Middle East) at MacDill Air Force Base in Tampa, thirty miles from where I live. Since I knew of two local broadcasters who went to the Middle East and took a film crew, this could not have applied to broadcast when it was stated. Their trip made national news, so it was *probably* not a thing many television crews did. (**That last line is Editorial Assumption based on *known* facts.**)

The military officer I spoke with, who was stationed at MacDill, AFB, told me, "All the news stories that came out of Operation Desert

Storm were bylined out of only three cities. That's because that's where the media tents were set up for reporters to drink martinis and lounge in air conditioning until the military officials gave them public service announcements which were to be used as the basis for writing their news stories."

I know there is a good argument for not releasing too much military information. But we should be able to hear where the stories originated, and reporters should not be limited to PSAs for information broadcast worldwide.

Large corporations often keep news from getting out that would hurt their image as well. For example, in 1998, *ABC News* rejected the airing on *20/20* done by its leading investigative team because it reflected poorly on the working conditions of employees at ABC's parent company, Disney.

As reported in *The New York Times,* Eileen Murphy, as ABC spokeswoman, said only that the report was rejected because "it did not work out." As of September 2021, when I last checked, this story was still available to read at www.nytimes.com/1998/10/15/us/abc-shelves-report-on-parent-disney.html[1]

So, who provides what we see and hear? The people, corporations, and PACs behind the stations we listen to, with few exceptions like the online "new" Angel Funded, *The Flip Side,* which daily provides content in two boxes next to each other: The Republican and the Democrat view of each issue discussed. So far, I have seen no bias there and can find funding only from private persons, with three levels of giving allowed: $1 a month, $3 a month, and $10 a month.

I know others are still fighting to publicize the truth too, and in our last chapter, we will talk about who some of them are and how to seek them out.

---

1.   http://www.nytimes.com/1998/10/15/us/abc-shelves-report-on-parent-disney.html

4

'Convergence'- What Is It & How It Felt To Be a Reporter in the Midst of It

To truly understand how the media uses the word *convergence* beyond its original dictionary definition, I am going to show a fictional scenario made up of things that actually happened, only with a different theme and in a different order. This compilation of events has been put together to make a very long story short and easily understandable. It may be a fictional composite, but these things are happening every day.

First, let's examine the *change in the definition of the word 'Convergence,'* which has occurred over the last several decades. This is the word most often used during buyouts or merging of more than one news source.

The definition of "convergence" is written in Webster's New World Modern Desk Edition Dictionary, published by Prentiss Hall Press, which lists the first copyright date as 1972 (followed by1974, 1976, and 1978). And yes, I still have a desk-edition dictionary. It says, "Convergence- The act or fact of converging. The point at which things converge." This brings us to the word converge, which this dictionary defines as "coming together at a point."

Now we'll go online, where most of modern society looks for definitions.

The modern Merriam-Webster online definition of that same word, 'convergence,' is "the act of converging; moving toward union or uniformity as in the convergence of the three rivers. Especially: a coordinated movement of the two eyes so that the image of a single point is formed on corresponding retinal areas."

The six words that stick out in today's definition that are missing from the earlier version are **union or uniformity** and **a coordinated**

movement." The wording of two eyes forming a single image is also precise.

That is just what is happening as large media buys out smaller media, gets bigger, buys even larger media, and gets fat. Then it rolls forward, taking everything it can pick up, as it goes as far as new rules allow it to, and even farther if it breaks up into smaller entities, all with different names. That is precisely what happened when large media started buying smaller media and got larger and larger so that now only a few massive corporations own almost all the news, whether read, seen, or heard.

Now for the compilation of several events I mentioned at the beginning of this chapter. Let's set this example in 1998. Here you'll get a little preparation for the full A-to-Z propaganda campaign I said you'd see in a later chapter, "An Example of a Propaganda Campaign & How the Voters Were Misled."

* * *

About twenty people sat in folding chairs in the building's small conference room. They were primarily long-time staffers, columnists, investigative journalists, and those who trained the newbies.

There was a great deal of whispering. The rumor mill was working overtime today. Just that week, they had found out a large, out-of-state company had bought their daily paper, radio station, and everything else in the area except two small hyperlocal newspapers that had been around for more than fifty years.

They had all known the paper was for sale again, but until the last 'I' had been dotted and the last 'T' on the contract was crossed, no one was aware of the finality of what was now being referred to as the latest merger. This was the first merger done so quickly and without strangers moving around the building and examining things.

Convergence and synergy were still relatively new buzzwords. But now that they thought about it sitting there in the conference room, those two words had been dominant in every memo they'd gotten for several weeks. Until now, most of the staff seemed to know when a buyout was coming. During negotiations, people were usually transferred, hiring and training stopped, and it got hard to obtain even the most basic supplies. Attrition ruled, although laying off wasn't usually done before a buyout unless it was in the form of early retirement. However, when someone left, they were not replaced, leaving the salaried employees working fifty, sometimes sixty, or even seventy hours a week for their forty-hour pay. The bottom line was always key in a sale, so sales were usually pretty easy to predict. But not this buyout. This time was different. *Felt different.*

Those who had been invited to attend whatever presentation was about to take place were imagining all sorts of things. Would they have to start working long hours for the same pay, or would hiring continue during the change-over? All the CEOs knew that these journalists cared about the quality of the stories that showed up under their bylines. No respectable journalist would go home until a story was finished and finished right, even if that meant working long hours into the night.

They had seen a tremendous cutting of expenses for a long time, buyout after buyout. For a couple of years, columnists and investigative journalists with large followings who used to have private offices had been moved into bullpens with the clerks who did the typesetting of Community Calendar events and Obituaries. For several years, it had been apparent that neither privacy nor community status was valued as they had once been.

From the memos sent out just the day before this meeting to staff members who were invited to attend, it appeared that the executives from the new company seemed to know nothing about news. Everything in the memo was about entertainment and "enlarging the base."

The new owners had invited about twenty highly-regarded and long-term employees to view a new public service announcement. None of them had any idea why only part of the news staff had been invited or why they would even be invited to view a PSA.

Finally, despite a heatwave that had most of the journalists in short-sleeve shirts, six upper-middle-aged men in jackets and ties came out on the slight rise that served as a stage when speakers were present. They all sat except the one who walked up to the small podium and took the mic.

"Good afternoon, ladies and gentlemen," the dark-suited man with the graying beard began. "We understand you are the backbone of this organization, the work-horses, the ones who make things happen here."

Work-horses, yeah, that's about right.

"Before we go into the main subject of this meeting, let me introduce the Board of Directors of our company. And so, he did, each one standing and looking out over the small sea of faces and then sitting back down. One gave a half-smile. The rest just stood up and sat down.

"You're in for some fascinating changes," the speaker began. "Some of you will be trained to go on camera. You'll find that synergy will allow you to stretch yourselves farther than you ever imagined. Those who will get to apply for the anchor desk should find their invitations in their email in the next two weeks."

Anchor desk? Did that mean they had been merged with the local television station?

What print journalist wanted to go on camera? It was certainly not what any of those present desired.

"But today, we want to get your opinion on a new PSA." He stopped for effect and then continued. "This type of PSA has proved to enlarge the base, the viewing public, by as much as forty percent in some areas. But each geographical area is different, and we know you know the demographics here better than we do, so we're going to take any suggestions you may have in hopes of improving the piece for your specific audience before releasing it."

Yep. They'd bought the television station. And something told those who were assembled they weren't being shown this PSA to help make it better fit their demographics. The feeling that was evident throughout the suddenly dead-still twenty-some chairs was, "this is the new way we're going to be doing things, and they want to know up front who is going to give them a problem with it."

"Nowadays, policing videos are vital," the man at the mic said. He nodded to someone who then started rolling down the screen at the back of the stage and then to the man sitting almost in the center of the stage and said, "Mr. Smith can explain this better than I can." He smiled at Mr. Smith and sat down. **Editorial Comment: Since this is a compilation of several events, no company name is used, and the name Smith is fictitious. Remember too that we set this in 1998.**

Mr. Smith took the podium without smiling. Looking straight ahead, he said, "Our videographers are experts in their field. We're hoping this piece will lead the news segment in all of our three-hundred-and-fifty-two stations across the country in about three weeks, with some changes made specifically for each market, of course. Our associates expect hundreds of smaller stations will pick up the piece from them too. You know, the news watchers. It's good for us that they watch the major stations to be sure they don't miss anything."

Three-hundred-and-fifty-two? Damn. So much for originality.

Most of the journalists in the room were immediately uneasy about the content of a PSA leading a news broadcast. But then, the lights dimmed, and their worst fears were realized. They were all aware of the news-watching process that accounted for the same pieces being aired on almost every station in large geographical areas, but it hadn't affected them directly yet. Often, the stories so many had in common were celebrity features like "who had just fathered some unmarried pop singer's child," instead of the dozens of important things that were happening around the world at any given moment every day.

A piece of the conversation between two men on stage was picked up by some in the front rows of chairs.

"Most of them are too concerned with what their place will be in the new focus to notice."

Those who heard wondered, Notice what? That the piece was deliberately configured to look like news, called a PSA, but was really some kind of native advertising, a new type of ad that was put in both print and broadcast to match the content of a news segment, so it fit right in and appeared to be part of the news programming?

From the title that stood still on the screen until the men on stage moved out of the way, it was apparent it was a gun control piece. These people knew others who had gone through this process after takeovers. They had been told about tech specialists who did subliminal embeds and others who specialized in choreographing background music that could raise viewers' body temperature and heart rate just by listening. But that was in broadcast.

How could this concern them? They were print journalists. Each wondered who would still be there and who would be gone by the following quarterly report. Something already seemed wrong. They remembered what their friends had told them happened at the television station. Subliminal embeds? Music to raise people's temperature and heart rate? *What kind of bullshit was about to unfold?*

Some journalists sat staring at the screen, which opened slowly to a picture of a little boy, about three. He was blond and smiling. His teeth were small and straight and very white. A wisp of blond hair fell across his forehead. His eyes were wide. They were a very, very deep shade of blue, just the kind of child's eyes that drew you into them, clear and innocent.

One man who had been on stage got up and stopped the video. "We have seen a trend lately to include different ethnic groups into ads." He hesitated and then continued, "I mean PSAs. We think that is an excellent idea and plan to put several darker-skinned actors into our next one." He paused, seeking the right demographic for Tampa. "Latinos, perhaps? Yes?" No one answered, so he sat, and the video continued.

Martinez looked at Garcia. What the hell...

The child on the screen began to move. A reddish-brown long-haired dog came into view and sat beside him and nuzzled his hand. An unseen narrator began speaking. "His name was James Corbett. His parents called him Jimmy. He had a baby sister, just four months old. His dog was named Rusty. Jimmy loved to play outside with him. The family lived in San Carlos, California, where Jimmy and Rusty could play outdoors all year round."

The picture of the boy's face got larger, and everything else in the frame disappeared, including the dog.

"One day, little Jimmy was shot in the chest by his eight-year-old cousin. They were playing Cops in the family room. Jimmy's cousin took his uncle's gun from the nightstand beside Jimmy's parents' bed. He never thought about it being real. He thought it was make-believe, like guns in video games."

The image of Jimmy faded out slowly and was replaced by two men sitting at a news desk. There was a map of the United States behind them. They read statistics of children killed by accidental gunfire. These were followed by statistics of people of all ages accidentally shot and killed by friends and family. Some of the journalists noticed the time period of the stats wasn't mentioned. That would have been included in any factual news story about a number of gun deaths.

The statistics were followed by editorial commentary, which was pretty much accepted as a part of news on many stations by then. "Guns in the home are dangerous," the commentator at the anchor desk said. "Guns in the home bring trouble and death. Guns aren't protection. They're the destruction of family and friends, of children you love."

Following the photos of the men at news desks were close-ups of dead bodies in the streets, bloodstains growing on the pavement around them. People were standing around sobbing, making comments about fear and loss. Flashes of anti-weapons demonstrators carrying signs demanding all guns be made illegal to anyone except police and military interspersed with scenes of grieving families.

Then, just in case viewers weren't yet convinced, a kaleidoscope of clips was shown of people whose family members had been killed with guns, both accidentally and with malicious intent. The reporters could tell it was staged— that none of the images or words were taken from actual footage. Yet pictures of men in city police and county sheriff's uniforms comforting bystanders and families of the dead flashed between the bodies and blood seeping across the streets.

EDITORIAL COMMENT: The one-hundred-and-fifteen fatal police shootings that took place between 2015 and the writing of the first draft of this chapter in April 2021, and the rash of mass shootings of 2020 and 2021 had not yet happened because (remember?) we dated this compilation of events, 1998 when the takeovers were beginning to make the most significant changes to news ever seen in this country.

Finally, the surrealistic, fast-moving images stopped, and one cameraman moved in close and fixed his lens on a grandmotherly-looking woman who delivered the PSAs' punch line. "My family knows the importance of getting guns off the streets and out of our schools," she said. "My seven-year-old granddaughter, Amy, was killed when she discovered her father's gun in his desk. All she wanted to do was look at it," the woman said, now holding up a picture of Amy. "Think about it. This could be your child. Your grandchild. Or maybe a niece or nephew or next-door neighbor. Think long and hard.

Then let your legislators hear from you. Make your message loud and clear. Guns in the home are a danger to us all."

The close-up faded away gradually, and the opening photograph of little blond Jimmy Corbett returned. As he sat there, alive and innocent against the dark background which had, by then, also reappeared. The words *Think About It* appeared one letter at a time until the whole sentence was strung across the darkened screen.

Then the screen went blank, and one of the men who were now making their way back up on the stage turned off the camera and rolled up the screen. For a minute, everyone was silent.

Was there to be nothing about background checks or illegal gun sales? Nothing about how to make gun ownership safe? They knew one thing now for sure: The National Rifle Association (NRA) certainly wasn't one of the big-money backers behind their newest company. But who was? Perhaps an anti-gun lobby that believed only the military and law enforcement should have access to guns? But if that was the case, why? Could it be peace-loving people who protest wars and unnatural death of any kind, or on the other end of the spectrum, a group that wants to be the only one with weapons so it can take over the country once no one has the weapons to rebel?

How would viewers know the difference between this and real news? This wasn't even a PSA. It was Native Advertising which was relatively new and so natural. It was created to fit right into a news broadcast to look like part of it. The question was, who do our new owners work for, and can we stuff our convictions and dedication to our profession deep enough to work for them?

The journalists immediately understood the new owners would be pushing an anti-gun agenda, but of course, they couldn't know why. Their only decision would be whether to stay on at their jobs when they found out. Buyouts like these were happening all across the country in the 1990s following the court cases that eliminated the Fairness Doctrine.

Jumping to the end of 2020, The Society for Professional Journalists (and other sources) reported that more than 16,000 newsroom jobs across America had been lost in that one year alone, after a good ten years of gradual loss.

New figures in January 2022 say 28,637 more newsroom jobs were lost in 2021.

Who had the choice to leave and who had to stay for the paycheck that protected their families, homes, health care, and lifestyle? At least at first, most decided it was not the time to make waves even if they disagreed with a new owner's agenda.

> • This is the end of the compilation of actual events from several different accounts and presentations rolled into a single scene. Besides making editorialized "ads" like this— Native Advertising— that fits right into specific station's programming to look like part of its news, other means are being used to sway public opinion in the direction of big media's owners, as we shall see in future chapters. Entertainment 'news' fills many channels with reality shows that have very little to do with *reality*.

5

Recognizing Non-News: Editorial Opinion

Native Advertising & Propaganda

*People don't have to be stupid to believe that propaganda, native advertising, or opinion pieces are news. They're designed to fool us, and most are made the exact same way as hard news, except that the piece takes sides, often without any statement that makes it look like that's what's happening. Read on to see how this is accomplished. The methods vary widely, and by the end of this chapter, you should be able to spot **Editorial Commentary** in its many forms.*

Native Advertising

The "compilation" in the last chapter is different than propaganda. It's the new kid on the block. Native Advertising is advertising made to look like content that belongs with the news or other copy in the publication or broadcast show where it appears. In the case of the gun control piece in the last chapter, it was designed to look like it was from a newsroom broadcast. Possibly it was even shown behind a news anchor desk between items of real news.

There are other ways to infiltrate "Native Advertising" into news, so let's go into a couple of those now.

Let's say a show is about dating, and the broadcast owners want to draw you away from a competitor of their sponsor. This Native Ad could be a "dating story" advertising for a singles' website but sneaking in another product too. Maybe a couple is out for a walk together and ends up with one of them saying, "I'm getting hungry, aren't you?" And his (or her) date agrees. "Sure, why not try Italian? Do you like Italian?" And their date says, "Yes, let's try that place on Main Street." They may even walk past the competitor and shake their heads as they approach the wonderful place where they will enjoy their meal.

When they arrive at their destination, they plug in the second advertiser, but it won't look like an ad, just a beautiful setting with people greeting them like old friends. Then the dating site "story" continues as the couple makes another date over a scrumptious-looking dinner. Native Advertising can be inserted into another ad like that one was, or even into a real "story," maybe even into a series you watch every week.

In print, this could show up in a story about a couple who has just rescued a dog from a shelter. Very possibly, it is an authentic piece about the shelter and how overcrowded it is.

Now the couple is in the kitchen, opening a can of dog food. Maybe it doesn't say anything about "bad" dog food brands, but in story form, it talks about a couple that has just rescued a dog from a shelter wanting the best for him.

One of them opens a can while the other person puts on his coat, getting ready to leave after the dog is fed. Usually, in a case like this, the second person will argue for a second or two, giving the person pushing a specific brand time to say something good about the product's benefits.

"Your coat's going to shine, and you'll be so healthy," she says as she puts the bowl on the floor and shows the dog up close, digging in.

"Well, he's happy now, let's go for our walk," Or to the gym, or to that fancy Italian restaurant they plugged a few minutes before.

But the point here is they don't even have to say anything. Just show the brand and the happy dog eating it. Remember, it's made to look like part of the story.

These are exaggerated examples because usually, the print versions of Native Advertising are a lot more subtle, and therefore harder to recognize. Most just look like they belong with the rest of the content in the segment.

It could be as simple as that pet owner getting ready to go for a walk in the park, but first, he says, "wait, I have to apply his flea and tick medicine." In print, the name would be printed as part of the sentence. In broadcast, the name on the bottle would be clearly shown. But know this: in many cases, the journalist who wrote the original story (possibly it was even supposed to be a real feature piece) did not know this would happen.

That's *Native Advertising.* Got it?

Now for just a little history about what print and broadcast advertising were like before all the rules went out the window. In the 1950s and 1960s, things like comparisons of products were not permitted in advertising. If two brands were to be compared in a paid advertisement, only the one being advertised was named. Let's take Bayer aspirin as an example. The Bayer bottle was shown, but the "bad competitor" was always just called Brand X. No names were allowed to be shown in someone's commercials as not doing their job or not working as they were intended to work. The company paying for the ad was said to do its job better than the rest, but competitors were never named or shown.

Cleaning products were advertised the same way as many over-the-counter home health remedies, like Alka Seltzer's famous ad, "Plop, Plop, Fizz, Fizz!" It showed how the person taking it got instant relief, brushed aside her old remedy, which was always marked Brand X, and ended with her smiling from the wonderful relief Alka Seltzer had given her from her upset stomach.

Brand X was never named. Is it any wonder there weren't as many lawsuits back then? What is happening today when brands are shown to be better than their competitors (by name) can legally be called several things, including product disparagement, commercial disparagement, product defamation, trade libel, or slander of goods; and practically anything that makes a disapproving statement about a product. It just has to show it in a bad light or in a way that could hurt its company. Litigation is rampant in this area, running up everyone's costs to hire lawyers, pay court fees, and do mountains of paperwork that was unnecessary just a few decades ago because there were different rules governing advertising then, just like there were different rules governing news.

Propaganda is quite different. The current online definitions for it are— including on Wikipedia, which is *not always entirely reliable* as a source, so when I use it, I check others. Often though, when Wiki matches the other definitions, it is easier to understand, so I use it in that case (like here).

1) Information, ideas, or rumors deliberately widely spread to help or harm a person, group, movement, institution, nation, etc.

2) The deliberate spreading of such information, rumors, etc.

3) The particular doctrines or principles propagated by a person, organization, or movement.

Following is a lengthier definition as found when searched further online. This one comes from Webster's Online Dictionary: "Propaganda is any communication primarily used to influence an audience and further an agenda that is usually not objective; selectively presenting facts to encourage a particular perception. It uses loaded language in order to produce an emotional, rather than a rational, response to the information that is presented." **Wow! (Oops, 'wow' is an Editorial Opinion! Did you spot it? I'll bet you'll be able to spot these things easily by the time you finish this book.)**

Propaganda is often associated with material prepared by governments, activist groups, corporations, religious organizations, media of all kinds, and even individuals pushing a particular belief or cause.

By the 20th Century, the term *propaganda* had also become associated with *a manipulative approach to something*. A wide range of materials and media are used for conveying propaganda messages, which change as new technologies are invented. They have included paintings, cartoons, posters, pamphlets, films, radio shows, TV shows, websites, and now, social media.

Also, from online definitions of more recent propaganda: "The digital age has given rise to many new ways of disseminating propaganda. For example, bots and algorithms are currently being used to create propaganda and fake or biased news to look true, and spread it all over social media platforms."

Some say foreign governments are responsible for this. Others say it's hackers. Still, others say it comes from U.S. citizens rebelling against the government. Red voters often say it's Blue voters, and Blue voters often say it's Red. Unless the person saying any of these things can prove it by citing a source you can look up and see for yourself, it should always be read or viewed as **EDITORIAL COMMENT**.

The last and more complete definition of propaganda may seem very close to Native Advertising and Editorial Opinion. Still, propaganda is different because it comes in so many forms besides advertising or opinion pieces, and *it is almost always used to smear (or boost) a person, position, or thing*. It can be a video, similar to the one made in the last chapter, specifically to influence readers or viewers' thinking about an issue. It can come as an editorial opinion piece, written to make readers believe a certain way. But it also can be presented as simply as a phrase, even a slogan in a comic book, that when repeated enough, is taken to be true even though it is far from the truth.

In recent years, since the change in laws concerning broadcasting, propaganda is often found on one-sided talk shows that pretend to discuss the issues but leave out enough facts (or all of them) on all sides of issues but the one they (or their financial backers) want you to believe. And they can say all kinds of untrue things about those who hold a different opinion. These pieces are intended to make viewers, readers, or even someone who hears a statement, think a certain way, as do Native Advertising and Opinion Columns. **But propaganda has the added intention of** *smearing people or ideas that think or believe otherwise, or just the opposite: to make someone or something thought to be "wonderful" when the reality is that things are far from what they seem.*

Native Advertising, propaganda, and editorial opinion pieces all want to sway readers and viewers, but they are all slightly different. They all want to make readers and viewers think what their corporation's owners want them to think. There are many like this now, and it depends on which ones you listen to that decide which side of an issue you hear— and therefore believe. First, let's look at a few organizations with names meant to draw in like-minded people.

The problem is that they are not always what they seem, just like items of a ballot initiative where checking "YES" often means "NO," that we read about in a previous chapter and will study in-depth in a later chapter.

Some of these (but not all) are deliberately worded to confuse readers or listeners and viewers. As I said earlier, for many years, it was my job to untangle the wording of ballot initiatives for the newspapers where I worked and write them in language any fifth-grader could understand.

So, What Exactly is Editorial Opinion?

The easiest way to explain this in one sentence comes from Your Dictionary Online.com. It says Editorial Opinion is "A statement of opinion in a newspaper or magazine, or on radio or television, as made by an editor, publisher, or owner."

That's precisely what it *usually* is, although it can appear in many different ways. Most readers and viewers have long expected this to be a part of newscasts as most stations and newspapers are known to lean specific ways, especially in politics. It's pretty easy to spot, unlike the other two, Native Advertising and Propaganda. Editorial Opinion is usually marked in a way that shows what it is. Maybe it is written by a regular columnist that people follow because they agree with what they say. Maybe someone stumbles across it, like at the end of political debates, where a commentator is giving details about what happened and then suddenly slips in something like, "when Jones gave those inflated numbers." Or, "he stumbled for words when talking about the war in Ukraine." See how easily editorial opinion sneaks into a newscast? That's not news. Statements slipped in like that are **EDITORIAL COMMENT, and sometimes it's so short and said so fast it blends perfectly with the facts.**

Thankfully, newspapers often have a banner across a page saying Opinion Page, and not only paid columnists but the public is permitted to write *Letters to the Editor* expressing all kinds of opinions. This is one meaningful way to allow for different viewpoints, as long as "Letters to the Editor" stay in balance, not only printing those that believe the same way as the newspaper's columnists, staff, editors, or owners.

However, in the last decade, some of these are sought out by the media, knowing what kind of opinions they will get, while relegating Letters opposing the views of their owners' positions to the trash.

Often even the names of organizations *appear to represent* a consensus of how the American public would believe. Let's look at three very briefly. They all seem patriotic, but their missions are not what you would expect by reading their names. Can we spot right-or-left-leaning organizations by their name?

I think not.

EDITOR'S NOTE: I chose these three not because I think they are doing anything wrong— because I don't— but because none of them has a name that tells you what the organization is actually about. It's the word choices I am getting at here and how words don't always represent exactly what we think they do.

The first two sound very patriotic, and many would probably guess wrong about their purpose if they didn't know anything about them. You would think by these names that they all represent *all* the American people's interests, not "portions of the population." But nowadays, it is hard to tell the purpose of any group by its name. The third organization doesn't sound political or patriotic. But its name is confusing unless you understand its story because it looks like it is against the very thing the organization represents.

I've chosen **The Federalist Society, The American Constitution Society**, and **Citizens United** to demonstrate.

Let's talk about **The Federalist Society** first. Who were the Federalists? Remember the Federalist Papers? The following definition (with some language simplified by the author) is provided from The Library of Congress of the United States.

The Federalist Papers were about ratifying the Constitution of the United States with written contributions from great patriots, including James Madison and Alexander Hamilton. You'd think anything named after these papers would strictly balance democracy, with no left or right leanings. Right?

Wrong.

The Federalist Society was founded in 1982. Its full name is The Federalist Society for Law and Public Policy Studies, but mostly now just referred to as The Federalist Society. It is an organization of conservatives and libertarians that advocates for an originalist interpretation of the United States Constitution. You would think this organization would attract people from all parties, but it doesn't. It has Libertarians, who believe in the very least amount of government (the very word Libertarian coming for the Latin word for Freedom) and conservatives, most of whom are now taking right-wing stances in policy. That's what this organization is about.

Of course, there is a lot more to it than that, I initially had four pages here, but readers can easily find all the information I took out on the Internet. Just type in the name of any group followed by the words "policy" or "meaning."

Again, my point here, which is not an Editorial Comment, is that you can't tell what an organization is about by its name.

Now let's talk about **The American Constitution Society.** What could be more inclusive and patriotic than that? Most Americans believe in the Constitution of the United States, don't they?

Most probably do, but this organization was created as a progressive alternative to The Federalist Society. Its mission is to "promote the vitality of the Constitutional rights of individuals; genuine equality in all forms; access to justice, democracy and the rule of law."

Although that sounds like the same goals as the Federalist Society has, it is usually known to take a liberal view. When the Federalist Society takes a stand on a political issue, you can pretty much bet the American Constitution Society will take the other side.

"Freedoms" can be, and often are, viewed in more than one way.

Last, let's talk about the grassroots initiative **Citizens United.** I picked this one because the words you see do not always mean what you think they do. This is not to say anything against this organization and is certainly not an Editorial Comment, as you will see once you know why I chose this example.

I'm mentioning it strictly to show words can mean two different things at the same time, depending upon who's using them.

The mission statement for this organization comes directly from the Citizens United web page. *Still, most Citizens United references do not refer to the organization but the abolition of a court case by that name that this group seeks to overturn.*

The organization's Mission Statement says: "Citizens United is an organization dedicated to restoring our government to citizens' control. Through a combination of education, advocacy, and grassroots organization, Citizens United seeks to reassert the traditional American values of limited government, freedom of enterprise, strong families, and national sovereignty. Citizens United's goal is to restore the founding fathers' vision of a free nation, guided by the honesty, common sense, and goodwill of its citizens."

It is not my place to say if this mission statement is "good" or "bad" because that is Editorial Opinion and would be marked as such. I am only using this example because when people see the name *Citizens United,* they probably do not think first of the organization but of the many television commercials, editorials, and even bumper stickers that say **End Citizens United.**

I'm using this organization to show that words do not always tell an accurate story and need to be checked out before believing *anything* since the elimination of The Fairness Doctrine. Remember that complex mouth full of words and court cases from Chapter 2?

So, are these bumper stickers and television commercials saying to end this organization? Just the opposite. They are saying to join forces with it to overturn the ruling in a court case Citizens United brought against the Federal Election Commission. On January 21, 2010, the Supreme Court of the United States made a decision regarding campaign finance. The case was called *Citizens United v Federal Election Commission* and concerned how campaigns could be financed. The court decided that the free speech clause of the First Amendment prohibits the government from restricting independent expenditures for political communications by corporations, including nonprofit organizations, labor unions, and other significant associations.

It was brought about when Citizens United wanted to air a film about a political candidate as an advertisement shortly before an election. The opposing party said that would have violated a 2002 campaign reform act.

In detail, this is what the case was about and why it is crucial to understand it.

Citizens United had produced a film about a political candidate before the 2008 Presidential campaign. It was a documentary scheduled to be released just before the primaries. In the documentary, several conservative figures discussed various "scandals" in which the candidate supposedly participated. It was illegal under the Bipartisan Campaign Reform Act because the ads were called "electioneering communication." Its producers went to the US District Court for the District of Columbia to get a declaration that they could show the documentary as a promotional ad despite the Campaign Reform Act that prevented it.

The case *Citizens United vs. Federal Commission* and its final decision at the U.S. Supreme Court in 2010 resulted in the changes in campaign financing discussed in an earlier chapter.

The finding of the three-judge District Court was that there was "no reasonable interpretation of the movie other than as an appeal to vote against the candidate who was the subject of the movie," which made it "electioneering communication."

The Supreme Court did not change that decision. Instead, it applied "the strict scrutiny test" for the First Amendment of the Constitution and said, **"corporations could not be banned from making electioneering communications."** For a complete definition and examples of the "strict scrutiny" clause as it applies to the Constitution, just go to Strict scrutiny - Wikipedia[1], and you'll see how they managed to change the law for this case.

They also used the Fourteenth Amendment to make their decision. Created after the Civil War, that amendment was written to establish

---

1.   https://en.wikipedia.org/wiki/Strict_scrutiny

who could be "classified as a person." The original intention was to give former slaves fundamental human rights.

Before 2010, corporations were legally referred to in the United States as "artificial persons."

People did not connect the intention of the 14th Amendment to help freed slaves to corporations even though beginning in 1886, a series of cases were brought to the Supreme Court by the expanding railroad industry, using it in cases where they (railroads) asked for "personage of corporations," in which the Supreme Court ruled in their favor, one case at a time. Their decisions were said to be because railroads were a necessary "communication" for the general welfare.

This precedent was not used again until the Citizens United case in 2010, but was one reason that justices said they had to vote the way they did. The entire Fourteenth Amendment may be read at https://en.wikipedia.org/wiki/ FouirteenthAmendment_to_the-United_States_Constitution.

But for now, let's get back to the point of this chapter: What do we think of when we see a bumper sticker or a flyer saying, "End Citizens United" or hear the slogans, "corporations are not people," and "money is not speech?" Do we have a clearer understanding of what happened and what these things really mean now?

In the 2010 Supreme Court decision, Justice Anthony Kennedy wrote the main opinion that reads, in part, **that there is no basis for allowing the government to limit independent expenditures.** His exact quote (taken from the ruling) is: "There is no basis for the proposition that in the context of political speech, the government may impose restrictions on certain disfavored speakers. The government may regulate corporate speech through disclaimer and disclosure requirements, but it may not suppress that speech altogether."

Justices who disagreed were John Paul Stevens, Ruth Bader Ginsburg, Steven Breyer, and Sonia Sotomayor. Stevens wrote the opinion for those who dissented that said, "The notion that First

Amendment rights dictated today's ruling is, in my judgment, profoundly misguided."

The four who disagreed with the majority concluded that the distinction between corporate and human speakers is significant in the context of elected office. They said, "Although corporations make enormous contributions to society, they are not actually members of it."

So, in its decision for Citizens United to allow the film to be shown, the Court stated that corporations and unions have a First Amendment right to spend unlimited funds in campaign advertisements, provided that these communications are not "formally coordinated" with any candidate. ***Essentially, this means that the political speech rights of American voters and corporate entities are indistinguishable.***

With this landmark decision, the Supreme Court overturned years of its own precedent, rendering years of federal law restricting corporate electioneering expenditures, and annihilated the statutes in twenty-two states that (previously) prevented election spending from corporate general treasury funds.

This Citizens United case kindled discussion across America about money and politics, and its ruling makes it contentious today. Though it is long and full of legalese, the portion of the decision that affects politics (and the ability to buy ads in media) is just this simple: "...the FEC is removing all prohibitions of independent expenditures by corporations and labor organizations from using their general treasury funds to fund electioneering communications." (FEC is the Federal Election Commission.)

So, the *End Citizens United* bumper stickers and television ads certainly do not mean what they say: End Citizens' United! They represent the exact opposite. The "End Citizens United" campaign wants you to join the Citizens United (group) in its effort to do away with the court's ruling on the Citizens United case.

The Citizens United (group) argues that the ruling, in this case, gives too much power to large corporations and the wealthy, who may now donate as much as they wish to candidates who support their positions, and perhaps turn these positions into laws. More on this will be shown under "Dark Money" in Chapter 11, *Follow the Money*.

Meanwhile, this chapter aims to point out the difference between Propaganda, Editorial Opinion, Native Advertising and the fact that words don't always mean what you think they do.

All these things have one thing in common: They are NOT NEWS.

6

Media Changed Politics After the Citizens United Decision

"The media is the most powerful entity on earth. They have the power to make the innocent guilty and the guilty innocent, and that's power because they control the minds of the masses."

Malcolm X

African-American Muslim minister, an activist during the 1960s Civil Rights movement, considered an extremist by some, who was shot and killed while walking on stage preparing to speak.

I deliberately choose not to use more recent references in many of these chapters and instead am leaning mainly on history because of the tremendous division in the United States at this time. Many books are being written about the differences in current Red and Blue thinking, and friends, families, and even religious congregations are being torn apart over these divisions. So, in the effort to allow people from "every persuasion" to see how we got where we are today in the media, I am relying primarily on events in the distant and some (like this chapter) not-quite-so-distant past. Still, it is pre-pandemic, and before the 2016 Presidential election, when the country's divide widened from a crack to a chasm.

So, let's start this chapter with the story of the Global Trade Summit in Seattle in 1999.

The national media deliberately shaped public opinion before any protestors to the summit showed up on the scene.

How? Read slowly, and you will see.

News media across the nation portrayed the upcoming trade summit as "good for the nation" long before it ever took place. It painted anyone protesting this summit as a quack. *The Washington*

Post published a story saying that "The World Trade Organization's benevolent policies would face virulent opposition." When you read it, it sounds like fact. It doesn't sound like commentary and is presented as a news story. But when you stop to examine the *tone* in which it is written, you can see the entire story is slanted to the premise that any attack on global economics is an attack on the good of all concerned.

Once the *Post* made its damaging remarks about the protestors at the WTO, it wasn't a hard step for the general reading and viewing public to assume that the protestors who flocked to Seattle were a bunch of kooks out to undermine world trade. The *Post* was making the assumption that this deal was designed to benefit everyone and shaped public opinion before the event took place.

Talking about how the *Post* deliberately shaped the WTO Summit story reminds me of something else that happened at that same newspaper.

For those too young to know, a story published September 28, 1980, in *The Washington Post,* titled "Jimmy's World," by Janet Cooke was a gripping profile of the life of an eight-year-old heroin addict in Washington D.C. In it, Cooke described "the needle marks freckling the baby-smooth skin of his thin, brown arms."

The story engendered much sympathy among readers, including Marion Barry, mayor of Washington, DC.

Barry and other city officials organized an all-out police search for the boy, which was unsuccessful and finally led to claims that the story was fraudulent.

Although some within the *Post* staff said they had doubted the story's accuracy, the newspaper defended it. Assistant managing editor Bob Woodard submitted the story for a Pulitzer Prize, which Cooke was awarded in the Feature Writing Category on April 13, 1981.

When the editors of *The Toledo Blade,* where Cooke had previously worked, read her biographical notes, they noticed discrepancies.

Further investigation revealed that Cooke's academic credentials were inflated.

Pressured by the editors at the Post, Cooke confessed her guilt, and two days after the prize had been awarded, *Post* publisher Donald Graham held a press conference and admitted the story was fraudulent.

An editorial in the next day's paper offered a public apology. However, the paper's Assistant Managing Editor Woodward said at the time, "I believed it. We published it. Official questions had been raised, but we stood by the story and by Cooke. The reports about the story not sounding right were originally based on anonymous sources. Primarily, there were purported lies about her personal life, told by three reporters, two she had dated and one who felt close competition with her. I think that the decision to nominate the story for a Pulitzer is of minimal consequence. I also think the fact that it won is of minimal consequence. It is a brilliant story— fake and fraud that it is. It would be absurd of me or any other editor to review the authenticity or accuracy of stories that are nominated for prizes."

Despite this defense, Cooke resigned and returned the prize. She appeared on the Phil Donahue Show in January 1982 and said that the high-pressure environment at the *Post* had corrupted her judgment. She said her sources had hinted to her about the existence of a real boy such as Jimmy, but unable to find him, she eventually created a story about him to satisfy her editors.

Following this event, Los Angeles-based folk singer Phranc wrote and recorded the song "Liar-Liar" based on fabricated articles, and the song appeared in her 1985 album "Folksinger."

In 1996, Cooke gave an interview about the "Jimmy's World" story to GQ reporter Mike Sager, who she had worked with at the *Post.* Cooke and Sager sold the film rights to the story to Trio-Star pictures for $1.6 million, but the story never moved past the script stage.

Cooke is not alone in choosing sensationalism over truth. If you remember my own story in Chapter 1 about how my headline and first graph were changed to sensationalize what went above the fold (what you can see in a newspaper box), you can see it is not always the fault of the journalist who wrote the story, but often comes from those higher up.

So far, we have covered how ownership and the slant of that ownership affects media and those working in it. We have also touched on a few examples of how pressured journalists are to "out-do" all competition, culminating in relating the Janet Cooke story.

Editorial Comment: It doesn't surprise me what Cooke resorted to doing when she could not locate the boy she was seeking. Thirty years ago, newsrooms were still mostly male-dominated, with women just beginning to become affronted when men said: "Go get me some coffee," or they got their rear-ends pinched when they walked by certain men's desks. And no, I would not have done what Cooke did. However, what surprises me most is *The Washington Post's* Assistant Managing Editor's defense of Cooke's story. It would have been more common for that time for her boss to throw her under the bus to make himself look better. (Bravo, Woodward! I can say that *only* because this is marked as an editorial comment.)

This chapter is about how media began to have more and more political influence after eliminating *The Fairness Doctrine*. So next, I suppose I should distinguish between that FCC document and *The Federal Equal Time Rule* mentioned briefly earlier, which applies only to political candidates and politicians.

The Equal Time Rule specifies that U.S. radio and television broadcast stations must provide an equal opportunity to any opposing political candidates who request it. This means, for example, that if a station gives twenty minutes to a candidate in prime time, it must do the same for any other candidate (for the same race) who requests it, and at the same price. This has nothing to do with The Fairness Doctrine, which, if you remember from Chapter 2, said there must be time for response to attacks made on-air and for equal time for other sides of an issue if one side has been presented.

Remember, too, that The Fairness Doctrine is no longer in effect, as explained previously. The Equal Time Rule only affects *political speech*.

There were originally only four exceptions to The Equal Time Rule. But rather than go into the original rule, I'll go directly to the words in *The American First Amendment Encyclopedia* and what it says about the rule now. It states: "The rule is mostly a formality today because of all the changes it has been through."

Sound familiar? Yep. Just like The Fairness Doctrine, it's on its way out.

The information found in the rest of this chapter comes from two sources, *The First Amendment Encyclopedia* and *The Robert H. McKinney School of Law at Indiana University.*

As you read the historical significance and gradual changes to this rule, think about the stations you listen to or watch that do not give candidates equal time or espouse only the "greatness" or "shortcomings" of one candidate or political party.

As you read through the history presented by the two sources listed above, see if you can find the exact point where whichever news outlet you read, hear or watch breaks what is left of the rule today.

Sit back and breathe. This one's scary because it gives credence to the quote by Malcolm X at the beginning of this chapter, and is also reminiscent of Adolph Hitler's quote at the beginning of this book.

Remember the massive Congressional *Communications Act of 1934* from Chapter 2 that put all forms of public communications at that time, including physical ones like railroads and public utilities, into the same bill with broadcasting? The same act that created the FCC, which was made to govern the portions of this (same) legislation that concerned radio frequencies? But radio frequencies weren't the same as railroads (the original rules for which had been created in 1889), and it soon became a problem to keep the pieces of legislation to only what they were supposed to govern.

Editorial Comment: The act was faulty from the beginning, but Congress had no way of seeing the tremendous changes in broadcasting from radio waves to television to the Internet and beyond. Still, the broadcasting "rules" made in 1910 should have been kept separate from the 1934 legislation. Congress could see this at once because, in the same session, it created the FCC to rule the broadcasting part. But from that moment on, there was a problem because Congress is in charge of free speech, and the FCC is in charge of broadcasting licenses and rules, which is a form of speech. (Broadcasters use words, don't they?) So, how is it possible to keep the two apart when they are tied together in the same piece of legislation? When studying this question, we come back to this problem again and again.

For now, let's go deeper into the Equal Time Rule, a separate directive entirely.

In the beginning, the Equal Time Rule only said that equal time must be given to candidates in the same race. The McKinney School of Law states online that its purpose is "to encourage socially responsible use of the airwaves by broadcasters." This explanation goes on to say, "If a station allows a candidate for local or national elections to appear, it must allow the other candidate to appear also."

The First Amendment Encyclopedia adds that "Central to the equal *opportunity* law is the belief that the free speech rights of a political candidate to engage in political speech before a broadcast audience trumps the rights of broadcasters to engage in private control over their broadcast facilities. Supposedly, the law prevented broadcasters from censoring an opponent's voice, thus ensuring more robust political debate and better serving public interests."

In 1959, however, when a political candidate used the equal opportunity law (note that the Encyclopedia uses the words *opportunity law* instead of *time rule here)* to make defamatory remarks about his opposition, Congress could see the advent of television made it necessary to change the rules, so it amended the 1934 Communications Act to include the following exemptions to the "equal opportunity" provision. Yes, there was a change of words here, just like **"privilege" and "right" were at some point interchanged in speaking of a journalist** not having to reveal sources. Remember that?

The amendments were: "Broadcasters are not subject to equal access obligations when a legally qualified candidate is included in a bonafide newscast, news interview, documentary, or on-the-spot coverage of a news event." This amendment to the rule explained that it was made to relieve broadcasters of the impossibility of providing free air time to every minor candidate.

But right away— in 1960, the "bonafide news event portion" of the equal opportunity law was suspended to allow the Kennedy-Nixon debates because the FCC did not recognize a debate under the exemptions as a bona fide news event. The First Amendment Encyclopedia says this was permitted because "the debate was not sponsored by a party unrelated to the political candidates."

EDITORIAL COMMENT: This set a terrible precedent because either they didn't care or didn't see that being sponsored by "someone unrelated to the candidates" could mean they not only "could," but "should" be sponsored instead by big dollars coming from anywhere. Only the "party of the candidates" can be proven to be "related." This means anyone else is *unrelated* and can sponsor the events. But I know I can't sponsor an event large enough for television? Can you? Can your organization or club? Of course not. We would need hundreds of thousands or even millions of dollars to compete with ads produced by billionaires, corporations, or PACs. And so, the campaigns were handed to the wealthy by a Congressional law that originally was "written for fairness to broadcasters."

In 1984 this "suspended provision" was "suspended." Yes, suspended from suspension. Look it up. And if that isn't enough to confuse broadcasters as to what they could do, the Supreme Court weighed in with a ruling that said, "broadcasters may exclude third-party candidates or other minor candidates from debates because debates are not viewed as public forums."

Editorial Question: If a debate is not a public forum, what is?

In 1971, Congress solved this confusion by enacting the Federal Campaign Act, which was amended to the Communications Act—remember, that's that massive piece of legislation from 1934. They then said the FCC could revoke the license of any station for "willful or repeated failure" to allow access to the station's facilities or the *opportunity to purchase* reasonable amounts of time. For the first time, the word *purchase* was equated with *fair broadcasting time.* By 1975, the FCC had ruled that the portion of the "equal opportunity rule that dealt with on-the-spot news coverage of a bonafide news event would now include debates."

I believe the litany of cases and problems connected to "air time" in the Carter-Mondale presidential campaign in 1979 (and other cases) would be easy for any reader to look up and continue to follow this line of events, but right now, in 2022 and forward, **what is essential to know is how the additions and subtractions from a law that was almost incomprehensible to understand, to begin with, works today.**

After inquiries and legalities were questioned by CBS, NBC, and ABC in the 1990s, the FCC changed the exemption policy by changing the definition of "use of a broadcast facility." By then, entertainment programming had adopted elements of news and current events discussions, and the FCC had granted "access exemptions" to *Today, Politically Incorrect, Access Hollywood,* and the *Howard Stern Show.*

Look them up. They were the first of their kind. So today, many claim these shows and others like it— including one-sided stations that continuously present from either a liberal or conservative view, giving no counter-points— are found on most major networks across the United States.

So, are you listening to one-sided news? Do you even know there are other sides to the issues you follow? And just as important, is the fact that when most journalists are sent these "slanted stories" from home offices in other states, they have no way (or more often, no time) to check their accuracy, so they can't even be sure they're true.

Some wouldn't care because they have too much to lose. Think about it. News jobs have fallen off tremendously in the last few years, especially following the 2020 Coronavirus pandemic. According to the global outplacement firm Challenger Gray & Christmas, a record 16,160 jobs were lost in the news media in 2020, a 13 percent increase over the last highest record of cuts in 2008.

The report says that canceling of events and business closures caused significant drops in advertising revenues, causing layoffs in large media, including *ABC, Buzzfeed, The New York Post, The Atlantic, Fortune Magazine, Tampa Bay Times, New York Times,* and many other daily and weekly newspapers across the country.

Businesses know to advertise where there are a lot of readers, listeners, or viewers. Are we watching the programs where we get balanced news or shows that are more entertainment than news? Worse yet, are we getting our news from Internet posts that may or may not come from a biased source, incorrect source, hate group, or foreign (or domestic) agitator?

By the turn of the Century, American politics had become a playground for those with wealth and power. This is not an editorial comment. Who can and cannot contribute to political campaigns and how much is allowed, under what circumstances and other factors are all spelled out at https://www.fec.gov/help-candidates-and-committees/candidate-taking-receipts/who-can-and-cant-contribute/, which is the website for the Federal Election Committee of the United States of America. It isn't hard to read, and anyone wanting to learn about campaign finance in depth can go there for regulations and other links.

But let's get back to the title and purpose of this chapter, *Media Began to Shape Politics Differently After the FCC Changed its Rules,* and the famous quote by Malcolm X. Knowing the history of some of the laws and FCC changes that led to the *Today Show* and others like it will help you understand why we have so much slanted news and opinion (passed off as news) today.

It may bore you or enrage you, but it can all be checked out online by anyone who wants to go deeper.

Editorial Question: How much longer do you think the truth can be found online? Will the Internet be regulated, and if so, by whom? The government? The FCC? The owners of the big tech companies? Private groups pushing propaganda?

Come on. I'll bet you have an opinion on this by now.

7

We're Not a Democracy, We're a Republic & Why That Makes a Difference

"If the time should ever come, when vain and aspiring men shall possess the highest seats in government, our country will stand in need of its experienced patriots to prevent its ruin."

Samuel Adams (1722-1803)

A leader in the American Revolution and one of the architects of the principles of American republicanism that framed the culture of The United States. He was the fourth Governor of Massachusetts and second cousin to John Adams.

It is important to remember that we aren't using recent examples, so the Samuel Adams quote doesn't refer to the attempts to delegitimize the 2020 Presidential Election or to the mass of people who entered the Congressional Chambers when Congress was beginning the Electoral College vote count.

Neither are we referring to the people who participated in any way in the January 6, 2021 event at the Capitol as "patriots wanting change," as they refer to themselves, because I said I would not use any recent examples which could cause more discord and division than we already have.

No, we're going way back to look at the difference between a democracy and a republic, how each operates, and how the people get to "have their say" (or not) in each.

This will further explain the way mass media operates today.

When I first learned the Pledge of Allegiance at seven years old, the words "under God" weren't in it. They were added when President Eisenhower inserted them. At that time, Eisenhower stated in a televised news conference that, "From this day forward, the millions of our school children will daily proclaim in every city and town, every village and rural schoolhouse, the dedication of our nation and our people to the Almighty."

He was careful not to mention any religion or creed. He just said, "The Almighty," and used the word "God" in his address as well.

This famous quote is recorded in history books, but I read it first in *My Weekly Reader*, which I mentioned in an earlier chapter. In the 1950s, elementary schools gave current events as part of history class in the schools I attended in Monmouth County, New Jersey. Then, in high school, we got to take civics classes, in which we also studied current events.

I noticed a difference in the education practices by the time my children went to school in the 1970s, and even more differences in the school curriculum of the granddaughter I raised from babyhood, who is now twenty-four. Because I raised children, then stepchildren, and then a grandchild in rapid succession, I got to see the changes first-hand, year-by-year through more than four decades, as they affected our public schools.

I know my granddaughter was in the *last class to learn cursive writing*. When I asked the school about this, I was told the new public-school curriculum replaced cursive writing with computer keyboarding classes. I know I am not alone in wondering how many years it will take for everyone who knows how to read our country's original handwritten documents to die? Or perhaps the paid private schools and academies will continue to teach it, and only public schools will leave it out.

Editorial Question: What do you think will happen then? I mean, it's anybody's guess, isn't it?

Now, I have to consider that my children attended schools in different states than I did, which greatly impressed me with what I got from New Jersey's education. I won't name the three other states we lived in, but their schools did not teach them many things —even by high school— that I learned before graduating from elementary school in 1959. Maybe New Jersey teaches that way now too. I have no way of comparing because I have been away from there for more than fifty years.

But let's get back to President Eisenhower's addition of the words "under God" to the Pledge of Allegiance. They were added during the years the US was in the Cold War with the USSR. During that time, school-age children from kindergarten through high school regularly practiced "duck and cover" methods in case of a bombing. Like that would have done any good had a bomb hit, but evidently, either that wasn't a known fact at the time, or the drills were performed to give (us) kids a sense that we could protect ourselves by following directions.

Lawsuit after lawsuit has been filed saying that those two added words to the Pledge mixed church and state and that children should not be required to say them in public schools. While that may or may not be true, that is not the point of this chapter. No matter what side of that argument we're on, we need to realize that getting the general public to focus on differences of opinion about things like "church and state," or more recently, "statues left up or taken down," "or Dr. Seuss or no Dr. Seuss," are smokescreens aimed at pitting citizens against each other so they can't see the real problems some have created by taking words from the founding documents that were initially put there specifically to protect future generations and twisting their meaning for personal advantage.

Remember as we go forward that all forms of media operate on the funding raised by advertising. Once the definition of corporate giving was changed, as explained previously, large amounts of money were poured into politicians who would do the bidding of those who donated.

Then those politicians, no longer restricted after the 2010 Supreme Court decision, obtained "other sources," including PACs that poured money into media that would spread their messages. In an earlier chapter, we defined a PAC as a Political Action Committee to raise and spend money to elect and defeat candidates. There is a lot more to learn about PACs that can be found at https://www.opensecrets.org/political-action-committees-pacs/what-is-a-pac. We will be talking about the site Open Secrets in the last two chapters, which talk about ways to seek the truth today.

Through slanted advertising and paid propaganda, the ties between government and media will show brightly in examples that are still to come. Let's go first to the title of this chapter, *We're Not a Democracy, we're a Republic & Why That Makes a Difference,* and gradually explore how that affects what we read, hear and view in our news cycles today.

Back in horse and buggy days, it would have been impossible for the people to travel to make their wishes known to Congress or even their state officials. So, the wording of the documents allowed for a representative republic where the people elected others to take their ideas and do the traveling for them.

But wait a minute, aren't the words *democracy* and *republic* interchangeable? Don't they both represent societies where the people are free and choose their rules and laws themselves? No, they are not interchangeable, although it is almost certain the founding fathers intended for the documents to work that way until times changed enough to change the way government operates, which comes up in a statement by James Madison later in this chapter.

In principle, it would be almost like that if the elected representatives did precisely what their constituents sent them to do. Still, once they're elected, they can do as they please— or are forced to do by party officials, as we will see up close in a later chapter— or are unable to do for many other reasons that would take another whole book to explain.

After all, if your newspaper or television channel can't exist without the money from its advertising sources, it'll just fold. There are no rules to prevent that.

It's the same when a political candidate receives a lot of money from a wealthy person, corporation, or Political Action Committee or from lobbyists that spend countless hours on some candidate, group, or corporation's behalf. Once they take their money, the legislators are then beholden to vote for things that benefit their donors.

Before condemning this on principle, think about this question: What if you got a three-hundred-thousand-dollar donation to build something— let's not use a "bad" example here, let's say for something good, like a homeless shelter— and then the person who gifted it to you asked you to do something, wouldn't you do it, especially if they gave you a promise to feed the residents in that shelter for the next five years?

Come on, you probably would. I know I would certainly try if at all possible unless doing so was against my personal codes of conduct, values, or the law.

Editorial Comment: A good way to stop that would be to prohibit *any* lobbying, PAC donations, or donations from any person or group of more than a minimal amount. That would give "regular Joe Smiths, and Jane Does" a better chance to run for offices, as well as keep those already in power from being obligated to anyone but their constituents.

But there's another reason besides the obligation to repay donors that some politicians we've trusted to do our bidding do things they wouldn't normally do. That's because they have no choice if they want to stay in their seat, and if they can't keep their jobs, how can they ever accomplish what they went there to do in the first place?

No choice? How can that be, we ask? Well, to illustrate this, we'll only need to see the three following examples.

Back when I was a reporter for *The Sun City Sun*in a large retirement community, and at the same time for *The East Bay Breeze,* that covered all the towns around it, I interviewed Rep. Dan Miller of Bradenton, Florida, after he had given a talk there about his first year in Congress.

Miller, a Republican, was the representative for Florida's 13th Congressional District from 1993 to 2002. I'm not sure when I listened to his talk, but it was some time after he came back from his first session in Washington, probably at the large Republican Club I mentioned in an earlier chapter. I don't still have the newspaper this interview was recorded in, but I know it is somewhere in the Sunbelt Newspapers Inc. archives. I remember this example as clearly as if I heard it yesterday, and you will too once you read it. It's impossible to forget.

Rep. Miller said he had wanted to present the issues that most concerned his constituents. He knew what they were. Yet in the interview I had with him after the talk, which was something I always tried to do if the politician or other speaker had time to stay, he told me something chilling I could never get out of my mind.

TOO MUCH TIME HAS PASSED FOR HIS WORDS, TO BE EXACT, SO THEY'RE NOT IN QUOTES. Shortly after I was seated, a group of representatives came to my desk and lay a stack of papers on it. They told me to sign it. (Evidently, it was proposed legislation.) I told them I had to read it before I signed anything, and they said (this is an exact quote), "If you don't sign what we put on your desk, nothing you ever propose will ever make it to the floor."

So, Miller signed without reading the bill and said this practice was a regular for newbies in Congress (at least at that time). This conversation stayed with me as closely as the quote I mentioned in the first chapter: "I would vote for a monkey to protect the (party) seat."

Then there is a first-hand example of how something gets added to a bill *after* most of the signers are finished with it, so they never see the add-ons before voting. Why would they? They've already read and signed it, so they've moved on to something else.

Many Sun City Center residents used their golf carts for transportation around town on its private streets instead of cars. Still, they couldn't cross Sun City Center Boulevard because it was really a part of State Highway 674 and the signage only said "boulevard" for a few blocks through a three-mile stretch in the central part of their community.

A group of residents approached Florida House Representative Spurgeon "Spud" Clements" (1928-1992) with the problem of needing specified safe crossings over the state highway for golf carts. He accomplished this in the very next session. After that, he was practically sainted in the retirement community. Many long-time residents still remember crediting him for giving them access to their whole community by golf cart, which saves them from switching from their golf carts to their cars if they want to visit a person or business on the opposite side of SR 674.

How did Spud accomplish this?

With something called a "tape-on."

After the bill had made its rounds and was headed to the floor for a vote, Spud asked to be permitted to add something for his constituents. Because he was well-known and well-liked in the Florida House, he was given the bill at the last minute, and he added cross streets for golf carts in Sun City Center. So, when the bill was passed, and only a few signers had seen his tape-on, residents of the retirement community now had safe places to cross the highway.

In this case, the representative's tape-on *helped* the constituents he represented. But it does point out that last-minute additions to bills happen, and they do not always benefit the constituents of the one who originally wrote the bill for a whole different purpose. **In fact, such practices may even weaken the bill's original intention, and the**

wrong representative could get blamed for the outcome, which is also sometimes deliberate.

Then we come to the third reason our representatives, local, state, and federal, sometimes do not represent their constituents. There is plenty of graft, greed, and favor-swapping going on too. Remember the part in an earlier chapter that mentioned Citizen's United? When someone says they are "for or against" Citizens United, do they mean the ruling in the court case that now permits large corporate donations to political candidates, or do they mean the efforts of the group by that name that wants to stop that practice? When they sign on a petition or agreement (for either side), do they always know what they're signing?

Words in documents do not always mean what they say. Sometimes, changes like going from radio to television broadcasts cause variations that cannot be helped. But other times, things are worded deliberately to confuse voters and the general public.

One good example I am personally familiar with is the Florida ballot initiative to ban coastal commercial fishing. Since I was involved in writing about that through the whole campaign, I will lay that one example out from A-to-Z in the next chapter to make it easy for readers to understand how a propaganda campaign operates.

This chapter aims to show the difference between a democracy and a republic and how that can affect media. We just read three reasons our elected representatives don't always do what we send them to do, which is how a republic should operate.

In a democracy, however, every eligible voter has a say in all the legislation, meetings, and whatever else they want to vote on.

We must realize that although our leaders and representatives use the word democracy in their speeches, it's actually the word republic that is used in most of our founding documents. Republic is the word that defines our form of government. Many intelligent, informed people think the terms democracy and republic are interchangeable.

Since they aren't, we will examine them where necessary to make sense of some things referenced in this book.

Remember the demise of much of the 1934 Communications legislation that tried to encompass everything in one package? Many citizens had opinions about whether the rulings that followed actually helped free speech, which was supposedly their intention. Some people even maintained that the courts' more recent opinions had made speech over the airwaves (and television screens) easy to falsify. Now, even when all sides of a multi-sided issue are given— which on many stations they're not— sometimes it is in such a way deliberately designed to form an opinion.

What do you think should have been done to ensure our news and other pertinent information sent over airwaves is accurate, and what do you think we could do now to remedy this situation if anything?

EDITORIAL QUESTION: Do you think it is possible we could lose our form of representative government through the use of media propaganda? Oh wait, I'm getting ahead of myself. We haven't gotten to the A-to-Z example of a propaganda campaign yet!

Our founding fathers were well aware that times would change, and the system would have to change with them. The fourth President of the United States, James Madison, is quoted as saying, "The day will come when our Republic will be an impossibility because wealth will be concentrated in the hands of a few. When that day comes, we must rely on the wisdom of the best elements in the country to readjust the laws of the nation."

Again, I am not referring to any type of "coup," succession, or division like the January 6, 2021 attack on the US Capitol. I am referring to change in government by the people, as Madison intended when he stated, "we must rely on the wisdom of the *best elements* of the country to readjust the laws of the nation." The best element cannot be irrational, biased, or ruled by $$$, but by

persons who wish to assure the "Liberty and Justice for all" for which Madison and our other founders intended.

This statement proves the founding fathers and first Presidents knew we would have to change our system as time went on. Still, there are reasons why we can't just jump into a one-person, one-vote system even though our technology can now handle it. Before we dare to do something like that, we would have to find a way to rule out the injustices that might be done to specific groups or individuals by a majority because we can't legislate what that majority might do.

What if we allowed states to make their own rules (the old argument of states' rights again) and one state wanted to commit genocide or adopt some new cruel and inhuman punishment on specific groups of people? Reinstitute slavery, for example. Or retribution against those marching on Pride Day. Or perhaps outlawing women from politics or giving prizes for the number of exotic animals hunted and killed?

How fair would the States' Rights argument be to *all* the people then?

This was one of the things the founding fathers were trying to prevent by applying the principles of American Republicanism. (Again, this has nothing to do with the Republican Party.) So, let's examine what it does mean.

Republicanism has been the guiding political philosophy of the United States since its beginning. It stresses "liberty and inalienable rights" as central values, makes people as a whole "sovereign," rejects aristocracy (kings, queens, and other ruling families) as well as any other type of inherited power.

True republicanism expects its citizens to be independent in their performance of civic duties and criticizes all forms of government corruption.

Republicanism is an ideology based on Ancient Greco-Roman, Renaissance, and English models and ideas. You can read about this adoption of ideas in depth at Republicanism in the United States - Wikipedia[1]. It formed the basis for the American Revolution and the Declaration of Independence in 1776; the Constitution in 1787; and framed the wording of President Lincoln's Gettysburg Address in 1863. The word republicanism itself is derived from "republic," and since it is the basis of the founding fathers' thinking, it was meant to promote freedom for all citizens.

So, if we have a government set up to represent us, and we do not feel the representatives we have elected are doing that, we have to find a way to change the representatives or change the system.

But how can we even know what the truth is when we only listen to "slanted media?"

Think about the news sources you read, listen to, or watch. Do you seek sources that give many sides to issues, or tune in to those that fit your belief system, or even to those that denigrate belief systems other than your own?

There are plenty of media around that do just that because of who is financing it. Remember the hypothetical hundreds of thousands of dollars someone gave you for that homeless shelter several pages back? Think what would happen if they called you for a favor a year later? Oh, it would be easy if what they asked you to do went along with your belief system. Suppose it didn't make you violate any personal codes. But what would you do if it went against what you knew was right?

It's easy to say you would stand up to them until you're watching your bottom line turning from black to red and losing everything you've worked so hard to build. It happens.

Unfortunately, it happens every day, and media coverage of it is badly lacking.

---

1.   https://en.wikipedia.org/wiki/Republicanism_in_the_United_States

8

An Example of a Propaganda Campaign & How the Voters Were Misled

"The media, stenographers to power."
Amy Goodman (1957—)

Broadcast journalist, syndicated columnist, investigative reporter and author, with twenty years, covering changes in America. This quote is found in the online version of the Encyclopedia Britannica.

Remember the chapter on Convergence and the compilation of several meetings I gave to describe how it felt during a buyout when you knew you were losing your right to print what you had seen and heard the way it had actually occurred? Well, this is the true story I promised to give you then. I covered a real A-to-Z example of a propaganda campaign that people only realized was propaganda two decades later, no matter how hard some of us tried to tell them while it was happening.

So much heavy-duty advertising money was pumped into the large media outlets that the smaller, local outlets that knew the truth couldn't fight against it.

First, let me explain that as a local journalist, I often became involved in news stories entirely by accident as I stumbled on things I saw and heard said on the streets and towns in my coverage area, which was also where I lived.

Once, my youngest son's high school football coach, who taught agriculture at a local prison one day a week, told me the warden there, John Doe (name changed), was aware that the meat meant for prisoners was being sold out the back door. This happened at the former Hillsborough Correctional Institution on State Road 674 in Riverview, Florida.

Looking back, from the age my youngest son was when he played high school football, this happened about thirty years ago.

I investigated and met with Warden Doe four times, and by my third visit was getting notes from inmates smuggled to me at the gate when I drove in and out. I wrote several stories about it while I was a reporter and editor for Sunbelt Newspapers Inc., **which I doubt (Editorial Commentary alert)** would have been permitted after the next buyout. Soon after that, Warden Doe was transferred, and later the complex was turned into a faith-based prison for women.

Many women I went to church with volunteered there after that, and from what I heard, things had changed quite a bit for the better. So, I wrote about many new programs initiated by the volunteers and how they were making a difference in the lives of the inmates. The kind of pieces we called *friendly, feel-good* stories.

Another story I stumbled upon happened while I was in the process of adopting a granddaughter. As part of the legalities, I was waiting in the Florida Department of Children and Families office, where caseworkers and their supervisors decide foster care, family caregiver status, and adoptions, and either deny the requests or prepare cases to go forward in Family Court.

While waiting to see a counselor, I picked up a pamphlet from Tallahassee, our State Capitol, and read an article about considerable funding for child care centers that had recently been sent to towns listed by zip codes, four of which were in my coverage area. State funding for child care in those areas? I hadn't heard anything about it. In fact, in searching for daycare centers for my granddaughter, I had heard many owners and operators talking about a severe lack of funds.

I checked into it and eventually ended up with a story that the zip codes had been incorrectly listed, and while writing it, stumbled on another story that led to an interview with Florida's State Representative Charlie Crist (around 2001), during which I learned about a health plan called Cover Florida that was being discussed in Tallahassee that I later also wrote about.

That story, *"Seek and Ye Shall Find,"* won a Florida Press award in its News Feature Category the following year.

I told you these things to show how local reporters can just stumble on news. It's always good to have people reporting in their home areas because they see and hear what's going on around them daily, and they have to be responsible for how they write their stories if they expect to keep living there.

In 1992 I stumbled on a campaign to put Florida's Gulf Coast commercial fishermen out of business, clearing the coastline for tourism, but it wasn't worded that way. It was framed as a campaign to stop horrific practices that killed birds and dolphins and turtles and ruined the Bay and the Gulf waters and surrounding environment.

As was later proven by marine-life studies, it wasn't commercial fishing depleting the stocks at all. The horrific images of sea life (apparently) strangling in nets used in television ads were actually taken during the tagging of certain species for a marine laboratory so it could follow migration, spawning, and other habits. But that didn't come out in the heavy-weight media for more than fifteen years after a vote had put local commercial fishermen out of business.

I stumbled upon this story just like I had the prison story, daycare story, and award-winning health program story.

This time, however, my family was involved. Before anybody jumps to conclusions about my ability to follow this issue without writing anything slanted, we'll start with *why* I felt I had to write about it. I knew I already had most of the pieces of the story before anyone else had even started writing about it.

My late husband and two of our sons were commercial fishing for a living at the time, following in the footsteps of my late husband's father, who had moved from Georgia to Florida when this part of the Gulf Coast was little more than swampland. I knew all about the nets and boats and equipment used for net fishing, how much different species sold for, and how many area families had done it for generations.

I had also written extensively about the netters and their lifestyle while a freelance photojournalist for the Outdoor Section of *The Tampa Tribune,* when I first moved to Tampa Bay, before taking a full-time position at *Sunbelt Newspapers* where I also covered new area development.

Because of the rezoning and County Commission meetings that went with the County beat at Sunbelt, I knew we were about to see an explosion of new people, both as a tourist destination and a through the flood of newly-permitted housing developments.

For years, well before our Gulf Coast area became what it is today, its primary industries were vegetables, orange groves, cattle and dairy, timber, and commercial fishing. One of the communities on my beat, the small town of Ruskin, had signs on both sides of the US highway running from north-to-south through it that said, "Ruskin Florida-America's Salad Bowl."

In the mid-to-late-1980s, the area's focus shifted. Permits began flying from our county offices to developers for everything from sizeable single-family home developments to townhouses, condos, apartments, and malls. Sold signs lined country roads, and zoning change meetings were long and often contentious, sometimes lasting well after 10 P.M.

Because my family was in the commercial fishing industry, I knew I had to be very careful not to allow myself to write anything slanted, and I didn't. But I knew where to look for facts. I knew it wasn't commercial fishing killing the stocks but the growing recreational fishing, and I could prove it with statistics from marine laboratories and state sources.

It didn't help.

A brief recap of the events in the order they occurred follows that will explain that last statement. Since only facts are included, I am not marking this section as Editorial Opinion, even though my family was involved.

* * *

In 1991, Karl Wickstrom, founder and publisher of *Florida Sportsman Magazine,* founded and became chairman of Save Our Sealife, mainly referred to in print as SOS. That same year, he began printing articles and photographs about how commercial netting was endangering the environment and killing sea life.

SOS began recruiting members from chambers of commerce and other business meetings who would benefit most from heavier tourism in the fifty-mile-long strip of land between Tampa and the next largest cities to the south. Abutting those fifty miles of coastline, thousands of inland acres were filled with crops, cows, citrus groves, and miles and miles of vacant land.

The group behind what became Amendment 3 to ban inshore net fishing on the 1992 ballot said the net fishermen would be permitted to fish three miles offshore, but none of the inshore netters had boats and equipment that could go that far out. The ads also claimed the fishermen would be compensated for their boats, nets, and equipment but did not consider the many different types of equipment and boats generations of these families had built up over time. Some had three or four boats, additional nets, and even motors for fishing in various seasons. But those writing for the ballot initiative made it look like those losing their right to fish in the only areas their equipment was designed for would all be fully compensated for everything they lost.

Their propaganda campaign made Amendment 3 look like a "Win-Win" for everybody. Especially the environment.

Television ads came practically non-stop, showing fish, large turtles, birds, and dolphins in nets. Images of sea life tangled in nets led the public to believe commercial fishing was not only cruel but depleted many species' stocks and destroyed the surrounding environment.

The words, "Stop the killing! Vote yes on Amendment 3," were always accompanied by videos of struggling turtles and other wildlife, some not even of native Florida species.

Other gill-net opponents, at first primarily developers and others who would benefit from a thriving tourist industry, jumped on board the ballot initiative. They said the gill-nets were wiping out fishing stocks and killing sea turtles, dolphins, and birds. Repeated statements and photographs brought environmentalists on board quickly.

The year before the amendment appeared on the state ballot, SOS, joined by environmental groups that believed the campaign was true, launched a press blitz. **Outdoor writers for five major Florida newspapers who wrote in favor of the net ban were also paid employees of *Florida Sportsman Magazine,* owned and managed by the founder of SOS.** So, editorials appeared in *The Tampa Tribune, The Tallahassee Democrat, Florida Today, Florida Sportsman Magazine,* and *The Fort Myers News-Press,* which later, in 2014, wrote a story about what had really happened, titled, *"Did the 1994 Gill-Net Ban Vote Mislead?"*

Editorials pushing the campaign also ran in *The Gainesville Sun, Daytona Beach News-Journal, The Sun-Sentinel, The Sarasota Herald-Tribune, The Palm Harbor Republican,* and the *Naples Daily-News.*

If these outlets had interviewed the Florida Fish and Wildlife Research Institute at the time, they would have heard them say that the most significant portion of annual fish harvesting was recreational.

The wildlife institute's records that I worked from noted that once new "bag-limit" regulations had been imposed in 1989, the area's recreational harvest of redfish had dropped from between 600,000-up-to-one-million a year, down to about 200,000; while the commercial harvest stayed at a steady 200,000, proving just how much more recreational fishing affected the species.

They went further, saying that commercial fishing accounted for about 1.14 million pounds of sea trout a year during the twenty years preceding Amendment 3, while recreational fishing totals amounted to around 4.4 million pounds.

But those few of us writing about what the research institutes and marine laboratories said were drowned out by more prominent outlets with more advertising dollars.

Not only did this ban put an end to hundreds of life-long— and in many cases like ours, multi-generational netters businesses—after voters approved the ban, much more fish had to be imported from other countries.

A brief explanation of the netting process will help you understand what this ballot initiative accomplished. It took almost twenty years for any large media outlet to realize and write about what had actually happened.

Gill-nets are large nets usually pulled onto the boat by hand, but sometimes over rollers. They're made to catch different species of fish in different seasons. Here, it was mullet in the fall and winter, mackerel in spring, and an assortment, including flounder, redfish, trout, snapper, and others in spring and summer.

The fishermen had different nets and other equipment for different kinds of fish, although some nets and equipment could be used for more than one species. Many also had more than one boat. The more experienced fishermen kept a lead boat, sometimes made into a houseboat where a small crew of four-to-six people could get some sleep and cook in shifts. This usually had a flat bottom with an inboard motor and carried large ice chests and other gear. Then there were the strike boats, with outboard motors that ran really fast so they could quickly circle a school of fish and let the nets down around them. Both boats usually had flat bottoms to run in shallow water, although the main boat that carried the equipment and ice chests sometimes had a deep-water V-hull.

The nets had leads on the bottom and corks on top that were put together by hand, including making the leads in molds in fires and then sewing them and the corks on with plastic needles made especially for nets.

None of the inshore boats were more than twenty-or-thirty feet in length, except maybe a homemade houseboat here and there, and the crews usually numbered from two to eight, depending on the season. It was always a small-business industry until the fish were sold to fish houses that resold in bulk to countries worldwide.

The boat owners were considered small businesses, taxed on the Internal Revenue Form Schedule F for fishing and farming, and were expected to give 1099 forms to crew members to file their income tax every year. The fish went from these small boats through fish houses where the boat owners were paid by the pound, and then they paid a "share" of the money made on each catch to crew members who had been on the boat during that catch. The fish houses then made the larger-scale sales, both in the US and also overseas.

Much later, in 2003, a study at the University of Florida stated the photographs in many of the ads shown during the campaigns before the vote on Amendment 3 were misleading because the wildlife shown in them did not come near the shore here but stayed far offshore, farther than the inshore netters' boats could go. But that was twelve years later, after the vote on the amendment that led to the commercial ban.

Later, some features and editorials were written about what had happened, including the story I mentioned a few paragraphs back, *"Did the 1994 Gill-Net Vote Mislead?"* (*The News-Press,* Fort Myers, January 2014).

PBS Florida Station WEDU, in its *"Diamonds Along the Highway"* series, even ran a feature about the old-style fisheries (Feb. 11, 2014) and how life, and the area, had completely changed after the gill-net ban, which by then, many sources (and journalists) had confirmed that the public was indeed "duped" on the ballot initiative by a richly-funded tourist campaign as I had laid out step-by-step in my stories back in the late '80s and early '90s.

Both Kevin Lollar's 2014 story in *The News-Press* and the PBS feature were done many years later, as cited above, long after everyone except the families put out of business by it had forgotten. I don't know Lollar, anyone involved in those reports, or any reporters who have written about it since. But I remember everything that happened, and it definitely fell perfectly under the definition of propaganda explained in the previous chapter titled, *Recognizing News, Editorial Opinion, Native Advertising & Propaganda.*

In 1992, however, shortly before the vote, I spoke to someone who knew the main photo being used to show sea animals trapped in nets had been taken in 1988 aboard the Georgia Bulldog as part of a tagging experiment at the University of Georgia. All the sea life shown in the nets had been returned to the water unharmed. I found this out because of someone I ran into at a fish house while waiting for my sons to unload their catch. The men I talked to said they had recognized the name on the side of the boat.

When the time for voting on the amendment came, only 2.8 million people voted to ban the nets, a tiny percentage of the voting population, which was approximately 13 million then. However, the catchphrase was "It was the will of the people," which made it so because it was proclaimed a victory in many television ads and newspaper stories.

In 2013, Judge Jackie Fulford of the Second Judicial Court ruled that the ban was a "legal absurdity and will no longer be enforced." Immediately, however, an online petition drive began, called "Reinstate the Ban," featuring words like, "Do you like Dead Turtles and Birds?" with a large photograph that was later proven to have been run on www.nationalgeographic.com[1] and had been taken off the coast of Brazil.

Still, in 2014, the First District Court of Appeals overturned Fulford's ruling, using that exact well-repeated phrase, "the will of the people." The same catch-phrase was used before the inclusion of Amendment 3 on the state ballot in 1992.

Remember that "By skillful and sustained use of propaganda, one can make people see heaven as hell or an extremely wretched life as paradise. Make the lie big, make it simple, keep saying it, and eventually, they will believe it."

Campaigns like this— especially political ones— that feature false information and rhetoric usually have a catchphrase people can recite verbatim.

My late husband quickly started another small business and recovered. Many life-long fishermen did not. If the things were reported had been true, I'd have never used this as an example of a propaganda campaign. They looked true. They sounded true. They made Amendment 3 look like a Win-Win for everybody.

Oh- the farms, orange groves, and cow pastures? They're gone now too. And the traffic here is heavier than in the City of Tampa, which made a recent list as having one of the ten worst intersections in America.

People have to go almost to the middle of the state to find crops and oranges and cow pastures now.

This is why I quoted Adolph Hitler again a few paragraphs back. One thing Hitler understood well was propaganda.

** Do you still remember the *definition* of propaganda from Chapter 5? If not, perhaps you might want to go back and reread it before going any further.

---

1.   http://www.nationalgeographic.com/

9

Buyouts & Closures of Hundreds of Media Silence the Voices of Many

"The day will come when our Republic will be an impossibility because wealth will be concentrated in the hands of a few. When that day comes, we must rely on the wisdom of the best elements in the country to readjust the laws of the nation."

James Madison

The fourth President of the United States and the person who worded many of the first ten amendments to the Constitution of the United States.

We just read that statement in Chapter 7. It's pretty important in this chapter too, so it's worth repeating here. The reason this quote relates to the title of this chapter about "silencing the voices of many" is introduced here and will be made completely clear in the chapter *Follow the Money.*

It's hard to imagine the United States as a country with only five radio broadcasting stations, but historical records show that's all there were in 1922. Yet by 1923, only one year later, there were five-hundred-fifty-six. Perhaps there were more stations in 1922 than the people keeping the records knew, or maybe the following year, a whole lot of people suddenly realized how powerful broadcasting was. Either way, broadcast radio grew fast.

The same thing happened with television. By the early-1950s, many homes in the United States had a TV, although they weren't yet common in the '40s. In the beginning, they were made with a tiny screen set in a huge box that was made to look like a piece of furniture. The first screens grew quickly from twelve to nineteen inches, but the boxes that held the equipment that ran them were often as tall as a chest of drawers and as wide as a couch.

I remember our first television well. I turned seven in 1952, and we had one that looked just like that. There was a tiny screen in a huge box. More people bought televisions every year, but by 1960, there were still only three major channels on them, and they went off the air before midnight, leaving only a loud, piercing signal and the company's logo on the screen.

Then the industry took off. Screens got larger, the boxes that held the screens got smaller, and new channels began to spring up all over the States. Cable television was invented to help with poor reception on farms and other rural areas, but it wasn't like what we think of when referring to "having cable" today. The history of cable stations is long and complex but progressed the same way as other media, starting small and gradually growing until the FCC had to set regulations on what it could do and where it could do it.

By 1983, fifty corporations dominated almost every mass medium. The buyouts had begun a race to own as many as the FCC rules allowed, and large corporations started to gobble up the smaller ones.

By1987, those fifty visual media had shrunk to twenty-nine, and by1997, there were only ten big firms.

According to Thomson Reuters' statistical information, by 2008, only eight companies dominated all large US media. Remember, this does not apply to your hyper-local stations or newspapers unless they have very recently been bought out.

The big eight left then were:

Disney, with a market value of $72.8 billion

AOL-Time Warner, with a market value of $90 billion

Viacom, with a market value of $53.9 billion

General Electric (owner of NBC) market value, $390.6 billion/ (But as of 2013, bought out by Comcast)

News Corporation, market value of $56.7 billion

Yahoo, market value of $40.1 billion

Microsoft, market value $306.8 billion

Google, market value $154.6 billion

Most still refer to the news service that supplied this information as Reuters, but in 2008, The Thomson Corporation bought the long-trusted Reuters Group, PLC. The Thomson Corporation is run by David Thomson, grandson of the founder, who currently holds more than 320 million shares of Thomson Reuters. His corporation also owns a portion of Refinitiv, a financial data provider, although it sold a controlling stake of that to Blackstone (a large financial investment management company) in 2018. Thomson also has a significant stake in Bell Canada and owns the Toronto-based *Globe and Mail* newspaper. Many corporations are now part of much larger corporations. You'll see that when you start looking at the news services you regularly follow.

In the chapter *Follow the Money,* we will see the names of some CEOs who avoid income taxes by hiding billions in offshore banks and billionaires who pour millions into political campaigns, right down to the amounts they donate and the amounts of tax breaks they've gotten. But right now, we're just talking about the voices that have been silenced as large corporations bought out smaller ones.

As buyouts like those I went through and others I described earlier, corporate-owned stations began to send national news to their subsidiaries, often with wording that is to be repeated verbatim.

According to *Business Insider Inc.,* by 2012, instead of eight corporations, six owned almost all the major media in the nation: General Electric, News Corp., Disney, Viacom, Time Warner, and CBS.

Business Insider Inc. is an American financial and business news website founded in 2007. Since 2015, a majority stake in *Business Insider's* parent company, *Insider Inc.,* has been owned by the German publishing house Axel Springer, which operates several international editions. More information about the six corporations named in the

2012 report can be seen athttps://www.businessinsider.com/these-6-corporations-control-90-of-the-media-in-america-2012-6

The article goes on to explain that meant there were only 232 media executives for every 277 million US citizens; one executive making the decision of what was viewed by every 850,000 Americans.

But then three of the big six bought more in 2018.

According to Thomson Reuters, AT&T bought Time Warner Cable Company for $8.5 billion. Walt Disney Company bought 21st Century Fox Inc. for $73 billion, and the mass media company, Meredith Corporation, bought Time Inc. for $2.8 billion.

And this set the stage for the biggest merger of all time, which follows:

When AT&T bought the Time-Warner company, it renamed that division of the company WarnerMedia to make it a different entity from its mother corporation. So, In May 2020, AT&T announced that WarnerMedia and Discovery planned to merge into a *new* company that would immediately become one of the largest media businesses in the United States.

Since WarnerMedia was kept as a separate spin-off company when bought by AT&T, it continued to own CNN, TNT, TBS, Warner Brothers film and television studios, and HBO. This meant AT&T could legally merge WarnerMedia separately— while it continued to own all those stations— with Discovery, which owned Animal Planet. TLC, The Food Network, and other well-known channels.

At the time of that announcement, AT&T said the new division would be led by Discovery's current CEO David Zaslav. In an interview on CNBC on May 17, 2020, Zaslav said the company intended to keep CNN and "go on to become the world leader in news." At that same time, AT&T CEO John Stankey put out a press release saying, "This merger will support the fantastic growth and international launch of HBO Max with Discovery's global footprint and create efficiencies which can be re-invented in producing more great content to give consumers what they want."

By September 2021, AT&T stated that this merger had been completed, but the new company's name had not yet been decided. These buyouts are happening so fast there will undoubtedly be more before this book even comes out.

Editorial Comment: This merger went through faster than either company expected when interviewed in 2018. This is perhaps the most important media merger to understand. With one CEO saying it will become a world leader in news and another CEO looking to provide more of the kind of entertainment consumers want, we can only hope there will be a clear line drawn between news and entertainment; a line, which has already been blurred in so many places across the country.

Just now, as I checked through the final draft of this book in March of 2022, it was announced that BlackRock Inc., an American multinational investment management corporation based in New York City, has bought many media stations and print publications, including13,896,606 shares of the *New York Times*. This is especially concerning to many as BlackRock also owns large investments in large pharmaceutical companies. I said 'especially concerning,' which is an editorial comment, but you can read the facts at: https://www.google.com/ search?q=Blackrock+shares+in+the+NY+Tmes&rlz=1C1GCEA_enUS838l

Also fairly new developments show that BlackRock is now connected to another financial investment giant, Vanguard, and both are now large shareholders in American media. Just look them up here: https://commonreader.wustl.edu/how-a-company-called-blackrock-shapes-your-[1]news-your-life-our-

---

1. https://commonreader.wustl.edu/how-a-company-called-blackrock-shapes-your-news-your-life-our-

future/#_853ae90f0351324bd73ea615e6487517__4c761f170e016836ff84498202b99827__8 future/#:~:text=BlackRock%20and%20Vanguard%20are%20two,Who

2.

Naming the most significant corporate mergers in the country doesn't mean there aren't others doing the same thing on a major scale. Those named in this book are just the largest as of the date this book was in the final draft. Following the links in the future we will certainly see even more media mergers.

In the next chapter, we'll learn of one company that has (or had at the time of this writing) 197 broadcast stations and still wasn't significant enough to have made the list we just read.

Numerous long-time journalists say they are concerned for their profession's future because media is pointing toward the Internet replacing television much like television replaced radio. Not "going away," just becoming secondary, especially as a news source, much like television is becoming less of a news source than the Internet today.

By watching the Internet, people can see that Bloggers, freelance writers, and reporters at hyper-local news organizations can often

53ae90f0351324bd73ea615e6487517_text_43ec3e5dee6e706af7766fffea512721_BlackRock_0bcef9c45bd8a48eda1b26eb0c61c869_20and_0bcef9c45bd8a48eda1b26eb0c61c869_20Vanguard_0bcef9c45bd8a48eda1b26eb0c61c869_20are_0bcef9c45bd8a48eda1b26eb0c61c869_20two_c0cb5f0fcf239ab3d9c1fcd31fff1efc_Whose_0bcef9c45bd8a48eda1b26eb0c61c869_20largest_0bcef9c45bd8a48eda1b26eb0c61c869_20shareholder_0bcef9c45bd8a48eda1b26eb0c61c869_20is_0bcef9c45bd8a48eda1b26eb0c61c869_20Vanguard

2. https://commonreader.wustl.edu/how-a-company-called-blackrock-shapes-your-news-your-life-our-future/#_853ae90f0351324bd73ea615e6487517__4c761f170e016836ff84498202b99827__853ae90f0351324bd73ea615e6487517_text_43ec3e5dee6e706af7766fffea512721_BlackRock_0bcef9c45bd8a48eda1b26eb0c61c869_20and_0bcef9c45bd8a48eda1b26eb0c61c869_20Vanguard_0bcef9c45bd8a48eda1b26eb0c61c869_20are_0bcef9c45bd8a48eda1b26eb0c61c869_20two_c0cb5f0fcf239ab3d9c1fcd31fff1efc_Whose_0bcef9c45bd8a48eda1b26eb0c61c869_20largest_0bcef9c45bd8a48eda1b26eb0c61c869_20shareholder_0bcef9c45bd8a48eda1b26eb0c61c869_20is_0bcef9c45bd8a48eda1b26eb0c61c869_20Vanguard

report things in their area online much faster than any licensed stations. This is one reason big companies are now vying for control of the Internet.

Well-funded investors buy up larger and larger corporations every day, and as you can see, the news is no exception.

Where once people worried about big government ruling the world, as in the former USSR, or as described as "Big Brother" in George Orwell's book *1984,* now single ownership of an entire industry is becoming possible through private enterprise. I would assume this is the concentration of wealth James Madison described in the quote at the beginning of this chapter. **I marked this as Editorial Opinion by saying, "I would assume." Does your news source do that?**

Someone with enough financial backing can actually "buy an entire industry" unless the government puts a stop to it.

It's the same as the candidate with the most donations in the campaign fund who can pay for enough ads to win an election, or, as we saw in the last chapter, groups can buy enough advertising to sway public opinion. That is why an earlier chapter in this book described the exact definitions of *News, Editorial Opinion, Native Advertising & Propaganda.*

How easily these corporate monopolies can influence politics as well. But as I said earlier in this chapter, we will visit some specifics of this later, in the chapter *Follow the Money.*

Editorial Question: Could it be that money could eventually make our system of Capitalism precisely what we fear the most: Dictatorship? We need to look deeply into these media buyouts and see who is actually in charge of the majority of the market share of each media corporation operating today. We are beginning that here, but mergers are constantly changing the media landscape. I hope this book can be a guide to help "everyday" people look into

these matters for themselves instead of taking their favorite station or broadcaster's word at face value.

Where once small-town editors would run down their cities' streets screaming "Hold the press" to include some significant event they had witnessed and knew everyone needed to hear about or see, now a few seconds of sound bite followed by commentary on what that sound bite meant is common and accepted as the norm by many.

Much that the public needs to hear is left out entirely if corporate CEOs do not think it will draw people to their print publication or broadcast station; or, worse yet, turn them away to read or view something else.

The most popular procedure on television news is to talk about an event quickly and then tell people what to think about it persuasively and at length. Some of the greatest news reporters of all time have issued warnings about this for years. But many of these great broadcasters and journalists have died, and the new journalism doesn't "look strange" to most students coming out of today's college classes. Remember Chapter One, where I got upset at my supervisor for changing the *tone* of a news story I had written? I had to explain "story tone" to many of the new reporters I trained for fifteen years. Mass Communications is not the same course as Journalism 101.

** This is a good place for me to say that I do not have any degrees, although I have almost twenty certificates from classes I took while working in the business. All my training came from specific courses I sought out and took; the companies I worked for, some of which sent me to classes; and other skills, strictly from experience. I worked my way from freelance writing for five national magazines and local news reporting to Bureau Editor in charge of hiring and training at the *Sunbelt Newspapers* chain; wrote a column for *The Tampa Tribune,* and on the side, edited for Amazon's first publishing venture, *BookSurge,* where I also learned to edit in British English. Later, I taught fiction techniques at the Center 4 Lifelong Learning in Sun City Center,

Florida, which was part of a seniors' noncredit college. By now, I must have privately edited about three hundred books and given my fiction class, *Write Your Heart Out,* about fifty times. In no way will I ever claim university credentials. If you remember, inflating credentials is what got Janet Cooke in trouble at the *Washington Post.* If she hadn't embellished her credentials from a previous job, no one would probably have even bothered to check on the existence of "Little Jimmy" when she won the Pulitzer for writing about him.

Now back to the subject of this chapter., *Buyouts & Closures of Hundreds of Media Silence the Voices of Many.*

There is much emphasis now on anchor desks, how things appear, and on following the instructions sent to subsidiaries across the country by home offices that sometimes even include the exact headline and wording of a story. If you remember, this is what happened to me after the buyout I referred to in Chapter One. Now it's happening on a much larger scale.

Some of the famous journalists who always did their own reporting realize this is a severe problem. In September 2012, Ted Koppel and Bill O'Reilly had a heated joint television interview. During the interview, Koppel said, "The media has created a political reality where Congress can't reach across the aisle," and blamed what he called one-sided reporting like "The O'Reilly Factor" for a slippery slope of news becoming entertainment and opinion that is more centered on persuading the public to view things a certain way than on the truth of what is being reported.

"Most news anchors are giving a flood of opinions to fuel their corporation's bias or their own opinion," said Koppel, who is best known for the twenty-five years he presented *Nightline* and also for his work with National Public Radio and Discovery Communications.

"It's become all-partisan ranting masquerading as news on Fox and MSNBC and a whole lot of others," Koppel added. "Once upon a time, we thought of journalism as a calling, and we didn't report on anything we hadn't investigated ourselves."

Koppel had issued a similar warning publicly on television about national and international news coverage when he received the Edward R. Murrow Award for Excellence in Journalism in 2011.

Most of us who have been in the field a while, have felt the changes he speaks of first-hand.

"We mustn't offend the advertisers."

"We mustn't offend (such and such) government official."

Censorship is real, and it is here.

Propaganda is real, and it is here too.

Politicians know it, make use of it, and allow it to continue to their benefit. This is not an editorial comment. This is a fact.

As the last draft of this book was being readied for publication, certain groups across the country were burning books that were once required reading for students in public schools. Their reason: The things in these books "might offend people." **The truth of the Holocaust, slavery, and the death of approximately 90 percent of the 60.5 million indigenous people who lived in North America before the coming of the white race should offend us so we never repeat any of those things again. These are factual statements and figures, but because I said "they should offend us," that part of the sentence makes this an editorial comment.**

Got it yet? Even using facts doesn't make it "nonbiased" if the intent is to sway.

Another rather recent development is the release of Harvard University's "Future of Media Project." This site contains the most recent lists of "who owns what media," compiled in 2021. In my beginning chapters, I said I would stick to older examples because of the tremendous division we already have in this country, and I will continue to honor that promise. But I do want to mention this source put out by Harvard, which says it is regularly updated.

https://projects.iq.harvard.edu/futureofmedia/US-media-index. This site includes not only the most recent index of United States media ownership, it also has links to names of both individuals and corporations and lists of where they send their political donations.

10

Politicians Are Chosen Behind Closed Doors

"The liberties of the people never were, nor never will be, secure when the transactions of their rulers are concealed from them,"

Patrick Henry (1736-1799)

Patrick Henry may be best-known for his Revolutionary War statement, "Give me liberty or give me death," but this founding father did much more than that. Besides serving as both the First and Sixth Governor of Virginia, he refused to sign the Constitution in its original form until a Bill of Rights to protect individuals was added.

This headline for this chapter doesn't mean our elections are rigged. It means who gets to run is decided long before any party even puts its candidates on a ticket. There are many reasons for that, but mostly it comes down to who has the money behind them to run and who doesn't.

We all know there are private dinners and events run by billionaires that are set up expressly to gain help for prospective politicians who would, if in positions of power, vote the way they wanted them to.

People aren't permitted to crash a wedding or birthday party, are they? Of course not. Well, private dinners given by private citizens are like that too. Invitation only is perfectly fine, and the hosts are free to invite whomever they wish to invite, including members of the media they know will report it the way the event-holders want.

In May 2014, *PBS News Hour* had a detailed report about a March meeting by the American Enterprise Institute. The lengthy and well-researched program showed that many wealthy business leaders had met with politicians at a private annual meeting on the Georgia coast. Still, only those who attended knew exactly what issues were discussed.

The meeting rules stated that only invited guests could attend, even if some of the attendees were elected officials. I am sure some of you are aware that twenty-some states have some form of "Sunshine Laws" that say if public figures who will be voting on a subject are meeting with anyone who could be affected by their vote, then uninvited guests (regular citizens) may attend. But many citizens of those states are usually not aware of these laws, and no federal regulation suggests such a thing nationwide. Anyone can type in their state and ask if an Open Meeting Law or Sunshine Law is effective in their state of residence. Who knows? There just might be a way you or your group could attend some meetings you don't realize you can unless they're *called* birthday parties or some other personal event!

Back to 2014, the year the *PBS News Hour* was aired, I mentioned a few paragraphs back. That same year, The Center for Public Integrity released a statement that showed a printed program for an April meeting of a conservative group's World Forum 2014. Names of those attending included House Speaker John Boehner and other Republican Congressional leaders; potential Republican Presidential candidates, New Jersey Governor Chris Christie, Wisconsin Governor Scott Walker, Florida Senator Marco Rubio, Apple CEO Tim Cook, Pete Coors of the Coors Beer Company, and executives from several venture capital firms. * **Yes, we're going to mention Democrats do the same thing!**

PBS pointed out many such occurrences where national and state leaders meet face-to-face with wealthy and influential people, naming three more similar meetings that had recently taken place. Organizers of the meetings told PBS on-air that "closed sessions like these allow the public and private sectors to discuss important matters from foreign affairs to tax policy and election strategies *off the cuff*."

Miles Rapaport, the president of Common Cause, a national group that advocates for less concentration of political power, said, "These meetings create more ways for mega-donors and elected officials to talk about shaping public policy behind closed doors."

Both Democrats and Republicans have come out against such meetings when the other party is the one that's involved because 'invitation only' get-togethers also allow time behind closed doors to plan what will be advanced by a large group and what will be frowned upon— perhaps even publicly denigrated.

Hold on. We're about to relate all this to media operations.... here it comes...

Let's go back to 1971 to the first example I remember clearly. That's when more than twenty million people took to the streets to demand that corporations stop polluting the air, water, soil, and wildlife. They also addressed deforestation and how corporations were "raping rain forests whose plants and oxygen production was necessary to life on Earth."

It was the first mass showing of what was then called the first environmental movement. One advantage to advanced age is having seen the things I'm writing about first-hand. I'm seventy-six now, and as I was researching this, I remembered seeing it play out. I just didn't understand the significance of what was happening then, and I'm pretty sure most other people didn't either. This was only the second time I remember environmental regulations being discussed in the news.

The destruction of our planet wasn't considered very newsworthy then and doesn't get enough coverage now. The seriousness of climate changes only seems to affect those losing their homes and land to wildfires and rising sea levels. EDITORIAL COMMENT ALERT HERE!

The first time I saw anything about the environment on television news was on New Year's Day 1970 when President Richard Nixon signed the National Environmental Policy Act.

History shows that shortly after that, corporate lawyer Lewis Powell, representing the United States Chamber of Commerce, outlined a plan for how corporations could survive and even continue to thrive despite coming environmental regulations. At the time, Powell was a director of several international corporations, including Philip Morris cigarette manufacturing. He wrote a memo to the United Chambers saying corporations had to organize and plan long-term and pool their money. According to history, the memo stated, "We must find and support activist Supreme Court justices to grant corporations rights."

That's an exact quote from the story that still exists for people who want to read the whole story behind this event. The story was still online as of August 2021 at http://billmoyers.com/content/the-powell-memo-a-call-to-arms-for-corporations/

This United Chambers organization is not made up of the kind of Mom-and-Pop businesses that most of us associate with the local chambers of commerce that are invaluable to small businesses and their communities. This historical information is not meant to harm them in any way. This is about corporate power only and was done nationwide with lawyers working with CEOs of large corporations.

Powell headed up a group to establish a National Chamber Litigation Center to fight for corporate power. Shortly afterward, in 1972, he was appointed to the Supreme Court by President Nixon.

Once on the Court, however, he proved his interests were not limited to corporate power. He pushed for more legal representation for the poor and often balanced a divided court. In all fairness to his memory, since his actions on the corporate power issue has a link above, I will provide a general overview of his years on the bench from the First Amendment Encyclopedia, as he is known for much good work as well. https://www.mtsu.edu/first-amendment/article/1352/lewis-powell-jr

* * *

American courts and legislation are not alone in shaping US policy. Worldwide organizations have a say in it as well. We won't spend much time on this one, but it is definitely worth mentioning.

The Bilderberg Club— also called the Bilderberg Conference or Bilderberg Group— is an annual private conference hosting between 120-and-150 political leaders and experts from industry, finance, academia, and *invited* media. About two-thirds of the participants come from Europe and the rest from North America, one-third from politics and government, and the rest from other fields. Each year, someone new may be asked to attend for a specific reason, even though they are not a usual participant.

The original conference was held at the Hotel de Bilderberg in Oosteerbeek, Netherlands, from May 29-31, 1954. Several influential people initiated it, and one of the main topics was the growth of anti-Americanism that was taking place in Western Europe at that time. As reported by the organization, the first conference aimed to promote *Atlanticism,* which attendees defined as a better understanding between Western Europe and the United States. It is recorded that its purpose was to encourage cooperation on political, economic, and defense issues. The words to describe its formation were "for a good and noble purpose."

Fifty delegates from Western Europe attended, and eleven Americans who were said to have been chosen by President Eisenhower's advisor Charles Douglas Jackson. The success of the first meeting led to an annual conference geared toward better relations and being able to speak "off the record" on matters affecting the world. The group's first conference held in the United States occurred in 1957 in

Georgia, with the help of the Ford Foundation, which supplied a grant of $30,000. Ford also provided grants for two conferences after that.

Without going into all the details, the most important thing to say is that those who attended credit the group's first meeting with creating a single European currency and the European Union. That's some pretty powerful stuff. More powerful subjects are discussed and acted upon every year. For example, once in a while, the group invites someone new, known to come just before that person becomes an influential position on the world stage.

In 1991, William Jefferson Clinton, then the Governor of Arkansas but not well-known worldwide, was asked to join a Bilderberg conference held in Germany. One year later, he was elected President of the United States. Then, in 1993, Tony Blair was invited to the conference and became Prime Minister of the United Kingdom the following year.

This seems to show there are a lot of influencers in this group. It has some hefty hitters from world financial markets and industry and politics. It's easy to follow just by typing Bilderberg Group into any search engine. But be sure to stick to factual histories and attendee lists because there are many unproven conspiracy theories out there as there would be with any influential group that meets behind closed doors.

* * *

Moving on to another way politicians are elected behind closed doors is hard to believe, but it's true. It's the United States Electoral College. Wait a minute. Please read further before saying that electing officials is exactly what the Electoral College is supposed to do. Yes, this is the institution that officially elects the President and Vice President of the United States every four years. Electors are apportioned to each state and the District of Columbia but not to U.S. possessions like Puerto Rico and Guam. The number of electors assigned to each state is equal to the number of members in Congress to which that state is entitled. Fair process?

Sounds good.

However, only twenty-nine states have laws stating their electors must vote for the candidate with the most votes in their home state. The electors from the other twenty-one states may vote however they want, no matter what their state's people sent them there to do.

What? They don't have to do the will of the people of their state?

No, according to information published in the National Archives, they don't.

That's hard to believe, but those in power know just how it works and play it perfectly, talking to each elector in advance and gathering to see who must be convinced to swing their vote to get a particular person into (or out of) office. And yes, money donated by corporations and the wealthiest individuals drives this as well. Sometimes, new districts are drawn up so that certain blocks of voters will be for— or against— a specific party or candidate.

This practice, known as gerrymandering, is happening now as it always is when elections are not decided the way some powerful groups want. It could be PACs, corporations, political party leaders, or any number of groups in power affecting the redrawing of voting districts.

I watched this done in Florida years ago, where a three-county district was drawn along the Gulf Coast that extended inland for less than twenty miles, just to put the coastal voters in one district and the inland farmers and citrus growers in another.

So big-money donors, heavily-funded private groups, gerrymandering, and Electors not having to vote the way their constituents want them to are some of the ways politicians are elected behind closed doors.

The last reason we're going to explore is obvious.

A candidate can't be poor. Oh, there are occasionally a few exceptions to the "wealth and power" in elections. Still, they are few and far between and are almost always someone who worked their way up over many years by being a mayor or County Commissioner in a local area and grew in power gradually from the support of constituents and local groups.

Think about it. How can someone take time off work if they have two jobs or one where they must work long hours to pay the bills because then there won't be any time to campaign. These days, that automatically eliminates most people trying to make it through the week to provide for their families. A 2018 study by the Federal Reserve (almost two years before most people heard about Coronavirus) states that forty percent of American families didn't have even four hundred dollars saved for an unexpected expense or emergency.

Forty percent. Let that fact sink in.

So, having money, time and availability are crucial before anyone can run for office.

Corporate executives from the country's largest companies funded legal foundations around the country, taking case after case to court in the 1970s and 1980s to say that corporations should have the same rights to donate to elections as individuals.

Between the Supreme Court ruling of the Citizens United case in 2010 and a 2014 ruling by the Federal Elections Commission in 2014, unions and corporations can now legally provide billions to a single candidate or cause. To understand the differences between the 2010 Supreme Court ruling and the Federal Elections Commission ruling in 2014 and how they changed the entire landscape of politics, here are two explanatory links by recognized authorities. The Brennen Center for Justice and the FEC.

https://www.brennancenter.org/our-work/research-reports/citizens-united-explained [1]

---

1.   https://www.brennancenter.org/our-work/research-reports/citizens-united-explained

Further explanation about how the two organizations' rulings are intertwined are found under an FEC explanation at
https://www.fec.gov/updates/mccutcheon-v-fec-supreme-court-finds-aggregate-biennial-limits-unconstitutional/ [2]

How many of us have read these explanations in a prominent newspaper or heard them on major broadcast media? I know I haven't.

Remember the description of Citizens United from a previous chapter? That's the organization that wants to overturn the Supreme Court ruling. Its slogan is "Corporations are not people, and money is not speech."

Does that make more sense now than it did when mentioned earlier?

Politics has become a game of "over, under, around, and through." If you can't climb over something or crawl under it, you can try any way you can to get around it. If all else fails, just bulldoze your way through it by throwing money and power at it.

Is that an editorial comment? You decide?

Oh, come on, you know what an editorial comment is by now, right? By the time readers close the covers of this book, I hope they at least know one new thing about how to tell facts from commentary. (BTW: That was an EDITORIAL COMMENT.)

As with media buyouts, many industries are now being run by those with the most money. During the last two election cycles, it has been reported by governmental agencies as well as private firms that one percent of the population in the country earns more than the other ninety-nine percent of the country's population combined. (That's the donor class.)

Now, if I were to say, *"That percentage is horrendous,"* that would be an editorial comment. Following it with *"that's the donor class"* is an editorial comment unless it cites a specific source. Yet

---

2.   https://www.fec.gov/updates/mccutcheon-v-fec-supreme-court-finds-aggregate-biennial-limits-unconstitutional/

that is the kind of thing most, not just many, of today's broadcasters and news writers would say at this point unless, of course, they are being paid by the one percent.

It is time viewers and readers forced reporters to return to reporting instead of soap-boxing their owners' and their own personal agendas. **That's an Editorial Opinion right there. Did you recognize it? Some are harder than others to see, especially when they seem to make perfect sense.**

11

Follow the Money!

"I weep for the liberty of my country when I see at this early day of its successful experiment that corruption has been imputed to many members of the House of Representatives, and the rights of the people have been bartered for promises of office."

Andrew Jackson (1767-1845)

Seventh President of the United States

This chapter will show you some lists of the wealthy CEOs and big-time individual donors who avoid paying income taxes and instead receive millions in federal tax refunds. All the sources of these numbers will be listed, one of which is a list leaked from inside the IRS, the source of which was under investigation by several national security agencies when this chapter was in its final draft in the first three months of 2022.

By the way— before we start naming these names— I want to be clear that everything here is completely legal under US law the way things stand now.

There will also be plenty of links to check out these sources. To start, I will cite some facts from ProPublica, Inc., a nonprofit news organization based in New York City. Its mission states that it is "a newsroom that aims to produce investigative journalism in the public interest."

In 2010, ProPublica Inc became the first online news source to win a Pulitzer Prize. Although it has a full-time investigative reporting staff, it has also partnered with more than ninety different news organizations to work on stories. Since it was founded in 2007 as a 501-C-3 (nonprofit) journalism organization, it has won five Pulitzer Prizes. To learn more about it, go to https://en.wikipedia.org/wiki/

ProPublica, where it lists its founders, CEO, Editorial Director, and more.

But for now, I will list the top three of about twenty donating foundations that keep ProPublica alive. The complete list may be found at https://www.propublica.org/supporters/.

It was founded by The Sandler Foundation, with a mission of contributing to independent journalism and the arts. Its second-highest two foundation donors are The Abrams Foundation, known for contributions to fair journalism, the arts, creativity, access to education, and aerial photography; and The Altman Foundation, which concentrates on New York, especially New York City's public schools and various other educational projects including early childhood learning centers.

Clicking the ProPublica "supporters link" above will give readers a chance to thoroughly examine the financial donors of all the organizations that provide to this news source if they wish to do so.

The point here is that ProPublica is not afraid of offending if what it prints leads to the truth, proved by its eye-opening stories, including the one coming up next.

In early 2021, ProPublica released IRS data obtained on thousands of wealthy people and reported that the wealthiest Americans "saw their worth rise a collective $401 billion from 2014 to 2018. But those people paid a total of $13.6 billion in federal income taxes for those five years, which amounts to a true tax rate of only 3.4 percent."

To read it in its entirety and follow its links, go to https://www.propublica.org/article/the-secret-irs-files-trove-of-never-before-seen-records-reveal-how-the-wealthiest-avoid-income-tax

The article points out that billionaires (and millionaires), unlike most people whose earnings come from conventional wages and/or tips, often benefit from "tax avoidance strategies beyond the reach of ordinary people."

It goes on to explain that their wealth is "largely based on the rising value of stock and real estate that is not considered taxable unless assets are sold."

ProPublica did not disclose how it got the tax information it cited but said the outlet "went to considerable lengths to confirm the information is accurate." It also published a paragraph in the article about Warren Buffett, CEO of Berkshire Hathaway. Research shows that Berkshire Hathaway owns more than sixty companies, including Geico, Duracell's battery maker, and the restaurant chain Dairy Queen. Although the ProPublica article states that Buffett's "true tax rate" was just 0.1 percent- which comes to $23.7 million of the $24.3 billion earned during the publication's five-year investigative time frame, it also states that Buffett reported legally taxable income of $125 million. This is not to say Buffett is "doing wrong," but to prove the inadequacy and unfairness of the way our tax system operates.

Editorial Comment: Buffett is known as a philanthropist and has given to many good causes. He recently gave away more than $2 billion and stated he intends to give away all his wealth before dying. The following link, dated June 2021, provides some information and also refers to other links that readers can easily access. https://www.forbes.com/sites/jonathanponciano/2021/ 06/23/warren-buffett-donates-another-41-billion-and-resigns-from-gates-foundation/?sh=75db95dc1bc9 [1]

Before listing ProPublica's record of tax evaders, it's important to read a quote by Philip Hackney, a former IRS official who teaches law at the University of Pittsburgh. According to the ProPublica story, he said, "I think this is big because it tells the story of wealth and the way it is taxed in a way everybody kind of expected but didn't know."

---

1.   https://www.forbes.com/sites/jonathanponciano/2021/06/23/warren-buffett-donates-another-41-billion-and-resigns-from-gates-foundation/?sh=75db95dc1bc9

The report also states: Jeff Bezos, founder of Amazon, did "not pay a penny in federal income taxes in 2007, and also avoided any federal tax liability in 2011."

The list continues as follows:

"Tesla CEO Elon Musk paid at a rate of 3.27 percent on a wealth growth of $13.9 billion. His actual taxable income during the five years (they studied) was $1.52 billion, and he paid no federal income taxes at all in 2018."

Michael Bloomberg, George Soros, and Carl Icahn were also named, with taxable income figures and amounts paid listed in this same report, as were other names less well-known.

https://www.propublica.org/article/the-secret-irs-files-trove-of-never-before-seen-records-reveal-how-the-wealthiest-avoid-income-tax [2]

Just click the link above to read the whole story, including the complete ProPublica-obtained IRS list.

At the time the leak was released, White House spokeswoman Jen Psaki said at a news conference, "Any unauthorized disclosure of confidential government information by a person with access is illegal, and we take this very seriously." Later in the same conference, she said, "The IRS Commissioner said today that they are taking all appropriate measures, including referring the matter to investigators, and Treasury and the IRS are referring the Office of the Inspector General, the Treasury Inspector General for Tax Administration, the FBI and the US Attorney's Office for the District of Columbia, all of whom have independent authority to investigate. So obviously, we take this very seriously."

Psaki also said she would not comment on any specific data in the article but did say, "Broadly speaking, we know that there is more to be

---

2.   https://www.propublica.org/article/the-secret-irs-files-trove-of-never-before-seen-records-reveal-how-the-wealthiest-avoid-income-tax

done to ensure that corporations and individuals at the highest income level are paying more of their fair share."

Ya' think?

Come on, Editorial comment alert! Television news anchors don't use expressions like "ya' think," so their editorial comments are harder to find. Just listen (or read with caution) to the way "persuasive" words get slipped into a news report, and soon you'll be able to pick them out easily.

In its report, ProPublica stated it "analyzed the data by focusing on the soaring fortunes of the country's wealthiest people in recent years and asserted they were paying a 'true tax rate' of just 3-to-4 percent." The news organization states it came up with this percentage rate by calculating estimates of the value of each stock portfolio and other assets and then sought out how much each paid in federal income taxes.

"This is *not* how income tax rates are normally measured," the report states. "Taxes are not levied on assets that are not traded or sold."

"We are structured unequally," said Hackney (the former IRS official introduced above). "The basic game if you're very wealthy is to hold a lot of wealth, let it go up in value, and generally to support your lifestyle, just borrow money."

Jeff Hoopes, a tax expert and associate professor at the University of North Carolina at Chapel Hill, elaborated, stating the following: "Since the tax system focuses on income, what is known as *unrealized gains* from unsold stocks, real estate or other assets (being held) are not known as income. These are extremely well-known facts. If you don't realize income from it that year, you don't pay."

Editorial Comment based on known facts:

Unfortunately, middle-and lower-income persons pay most income taxes. Many tax cuts go to those with wealth enough to back political candidates who will make more cuts and loopholes in the law. These people also pay expensive attorneys to hide money in offshore banks. This tendency has gone up since the significant cuts

to the wealthy began in the 1980s. At that time, lawmakers said the cuts were put in place to boost the economy.

As related to media, why do you think this goes under-reported? If you aren't sure, go back to the chapter on the declining voices in the news world and look up the donors behind your favorite news organization. We might all be in for some big surprises.

For now, we shall see some information from other government sources, none of which are under investigation. Everything listed from here on in this chapter is public record.

According to the Institution of Taxation and Economic Policy (ITEP), the following eighteen companies paid no federal income tax in some years (some in all years) between 2008-2015.

1. Pepco Holdings
2. PG&E Corp.
3. Wisconsin Energy
4. NiSource
5. International Paper
6. FirstEnergy
7. Priceline.com
8. Amos Energy
9. General Electric
10. American Electric Power
11. Ryder System
12. Duke Energy
13. NextEra Energy
14. Xcel Energy
15. Ameren
16. CMS Energy
17. Sempra Energy
18. Eversource Energy

Some of these companies are putting a portion of their profits back into advancing technology to effect planetary or weather changes, purify water, or other necessary efforts. Still, the reports say the average CEOs and high-ranking officials still make (on average) *four to five hundred times* what they annually pay their employees, and their expensive lawyers figure ways to avoid taxing it.

The following list is older. It was published in 2010. But it shows some of the highest-ranking CEOs paying no tax and receiving large tax refunds instead. It is not an editorial comment to say that no tax is being paid if a refund is given. This information is also from an ITEP Report that can be found online. All of it is quoted material but is not in quotes due to the list format used here.

1) Bank of America CEO Brian Moynihan received a $1.9 billion refund and $1.3 trillion from the Federal Reserve & Treasury taxpayer bailout in 2010. If not for offshore tax havens, the report states, income tax liability would have been (an estimated) $2.6 billion.

2) Goldman Sachs CEO Lloyd Blankfein paid zero federal income tax in 2008 and received a $278 million tax refund and a taxpayer bailout from the Federal Reserve and Treasury Dept. of $824 billion. If not for offshore tax havens, the amount Goldman Sachs would have owed is estimated at $2.7 billion.

3) J.P. Morgan Chase CEO James Dixon (CEO until 2021): Taxpayer bailout from the Federal Reserve and Treasury Dept. $416 billion. Amount of federal income tax that would be owed without offshore tax havens: $4.9 billion.

4) General Electric CEO Jeffrey Immelt paid zero income taxes in 2010. Taxpayer bailout and Federal Reserve money

received $16 billion. Jobs shipped overseas, at least 25,000 between 2001-2010.

5) Verizon CEO Lowell McAdam paid zero federal income tax in 2010 and received $705 million in tax refunds that year. It cut American jobs by13,000, the third-highest corporate layoff that year.

6) Boeing CEO James McNerney Jr. paid zero federal income taxes in 2010 and received a $124 million tax refund and $58 billion in corporate bonuses. Jobs shipped overseas, 57,000.

7) Microsoft CEO Steve Ballmer (who served from 2000 until 2014). The amount of federal income taxes due if there were no offshore tax havens in 2010 would be $19.4 billion.

8) Honeywell International CEO David Cote paid zero federal income taxes from 2008-2010 and received a $34 million tax refund.

9) Corning CEO Wendell Weeks paid no federal taxes from 2008-2010 and received a $4 million refund.

10) Time Warner CEO Glenn Britt paid zero federal income taxes in 2008, received a $74 million tax refund.

11) Merck CEO Kenneth Frazier paid zero federal income taxes in 2009 and received a $55 million tax refund.

12) Deere & Company CEO Samuel Allen paid zero federal income taxes in 2010 and received a $1 million tax refund.

13) Marsh and McClellan Companies CEO Brian Duperrault paid zero federal income taxes in 2010 and received a $90 million tax refund.

14) R.R. Donnelly & Sons CEO Thomas Quinian III paid zero federal income tax in 2010 and received a $49 million tax refund.

15) Qualcomm CEO Paul Jacobs: Amount of federal income taxes estimated would have owed if not for offshore tax havens (during the investigation period) $4.7 billion.

I am ending the information from the ITEP (Institute of Taxation & Economic Policy) report here, but much more information is available at https://www.propublica.org/article/the-secret-irs-files-trove-of-never-before-seen-records-reveal-how-the-wealthiest-avoid-income-tax

This is the same link that is referenced above. Once you get there, you will find many links within the article to reference the information above and more.

So far, I have stayed away from any statistics or references to the 2016 and 2020 elections, but big donors to the most recent campaigns will be linked (or listed) at the end of this chapter as part of *Follow the Money*.

There will be nothing else relating to the 2020 Presidential Election since that is what is causing the most friction between neighbors, friends, and even family members. So as not to contribute to any more arguments, I won't even touch on 2020. But to give the most accurate stats without going into 2020, I'll provide a few from the 2016 election, which most of us still remember. There will be nothing here about any person or party's "good" or "bad" policies, just figures; who contributed most heavily to the campaigns to give readers a better idea of how to *follow the money*.

Although many large corporations are known to fund politicians by heading up Political Action Committees (remember PACs from a previous chapter?), not everyone realizes the adverse reaction this has on the daily lives of the average U.S. Citizen. Since PACs exist on both sides of the political aisle, this is all stated as fact, not commentary. Both "sides" are participants.

Most people don't understand why it's so much harder to afford the basics of life anymore, whether it's housing, health care, clothing, or even food. They can't see the jobs being sent overseas so that corporations can hire people for a few cents on the dollar in sweatshops they keep hidden from the news. Nor can they see— or even imagine—the meetings that take place behind closed doors that take away Americans' opportunities to thrive or even survive. And this was before the Coronavirus pandemic. As of September 2021, the latest "Homeless in America" report released by the United States Department of Housing and Urban Development is on the following link. It shows California has the highest homeless population of the national count, 580,466. https://www.hud.gov/press/ press_releases_media_advisories/ hud_no_21_041#:~:text=WASHIN [3]GTON%20%2D%20The%20U.S.%20Department%20of,or%202.2%20perc [4]

---

3.   https://www.hud.gov/press/press_releases_media_advisories/ hud_no_21_041#_853ae90f0351324bd73ea615e6487517__4c761f170e016836ff84498202b9 9827__853ae90f0351324bd73ea615e6487517_text_43ec3e5dee6e706af7766fffea512721_W ASHINGTON_0bcef9c45bd8a48eda1b26eb0c61c869_2520_0bcef9c45bd8a48eda1b26eb0c 61c869_252D_0bcef9c45bd8a48eda1b26eb0c61c869_2520The_0bcef9c45bd8a48eda1b26eb 0c61c869_2520U.S._0bcef9c45bd8a48eda1b26eb0c61c869_2520Department_0bcef9c45bd8a 48eda1b26eb0c61c869_2520of_c0cb5f0fcf239ab3d9c1fcd31fff1efc_or_0bcef9c45bd8a48eda1 b26eb0c61c869_25202.2_0bcef9c45bd8a48eda1b26eb0c61c869_2520percent_0bcef9c45bd8a 48eda1b26eb0c61c869_252C_0bcef9c45bd8a48eda1b26eb0c61c869_2520from_0bcef9c45bd 8a48eda1b26eb0c61c869_25202019

The figures on the link are broken down by state, race, family status, and mental health in links found on the one above and taken from 2020 counts.

"The homeless rate in the United States has risen for four straight years," according to the HUD (Housing & Urban Development) "Annual Assessment Report to Congress" in early 2021. "Both the US Census, and HUD's 'Point in Time' Count, as well as the American Community Survey, agree there has been a rise for the fourth consecutive year.

Wow, 580,466! That's a lot of people. **C'mon. This is an Editorial Comment, even though it's a fact. If readers get nothing else from this book, I hope they learn to recognize the comments of reporters and news anchors that are made to look and sound just like news.**

Back to facts.

Right here where I live, about nine miles inland from Tampa Bay and twenty-five miles southeast of Tampa, many homes that were mortgaged twenty years ago between $550 and $750 a month have been repossessed by banks and are now being rented by those banks, not landlords, for $1,650 to $1,800 a month. This is a working-class, interracial, and multi-ethnic neighborhood that has seniors on Social Security, two-parent homes with children where both parents work, aging Baby Boomers, Gen X (1965-1980); Gen. Y Millennials

---

4.   https://www.hud.gov/press/press_releases_media_advisories/ hud_no_21_041#_853ae90f0351324bd73ea615e6487517__4c761f170e016836ff84498202b9 9827__853ae90f0351324bd73ea615e6487517_text_43ec3e5dee6e706af7766fffea512721_W ASHINGTON_0bcef9c45bd8a48eda1b26eb0c61c869_2520_0bcef9c45bd8a48eda1b26eb0c 61c869_252D_0bcef9c45bd8a48eda1b26eb0c61c869_2520The_0bcef9c45bd8a48eda1b26eb 0c61c869_2520U.S._0bcef9c45bd8a48eda1b26eb0c61c869_2520Department_0bcef9c45bd8a 48eda1b26eb0c61c869_2520of_c0cb5f0fcf239ab3d9c1fcd31fff1efc_or_0bcef9c45bd8a48eda1 b26eb0c61c869_25202.2_0bcef9c45bd8a48eda1b26eb0c61c869_2520percent_0bcef9c45bd8a 48eda1b26eb0c61c869_252C_0bcef9c45bd8a48eda1b26eb0c61c869_2520from_0bcef9c45bd 8a48eda1b26eb0c61c869_25202019

(1981-1996); Gen Z (1997-2012); and those following, now referred to as the Alpha Generation, because they will have been raised totally in the 21st Century. Some may see the 22nd Century as well. (I always wanted to look that up, didn't you?)

It would be difficult to find a more mixed middle-class neighborhood anywhere in America. It is considered a "nice" place to live but certainly not extravagant, has a community center, activities for those who want them, and a community pool.

I'm talking about my personal experiences now, so I see no reason to mark the following paragraphs editorial commentary. They are just things I have personally seen happen, written in the same conversational style as Chapter 1, *Who's Writing This and Why.*

I've seen several neighboring families lose their homes in the last five years. I have also watched Homeowners' Associations, here and in other neighborhoods, make rules forbidding multi-generational families and house-shares.

So, why do these people lose their homes, and some become homeless? Mostly because necessities have risen four and five times in cost and their wages (or pensions) generally have not increased. This is not commentary. It was a fact for people I have met, talked with, and watched lose their homes. One family I knew well lost their home because of medical bills. Another, for moving their children and grandchildren in with them.

Another example is when a homeowners' association levies fines for "lack of upkeep" (some things costing $10,000 and more, like someone needing a new roof.) When these things are reported to a mortgage company, that company can insist you "keep up the property" or lose the home. Just here in my neighborhood, I know of several homes that banks have kept to rent out rather than resell after repossession because the housing shortage here has driven rental prices so high. Yes, maintaining neighborhood standards is a good thing. But what happens to people who don't have the money or credit, perhaps from illness or job loss, to make the expensive repairs by the dates demanded?

They're losing their homes, that's what happens.

Arrogant people say these people are lazy. Some even say they're homeless because of drugs and alcohol and shouldn't be the recipients of charity. Yes, some may be on drugs and alcohol but have we become so hardened as Americans not to want food, housing, and healthcare for every person in the country?

I've seen some lose homes because of the nonpayment of property taxes. In another case, two older women had to move because they were house-sharing and splitting the bills. When you live in a "deed-restricted community," you can't do "whatever it takes" to keep your home. Many states don't have the abundance of deed-restricted communities like we do in Florida. But my advice is always to check to see if you're in a deed-restricted community before buying a home. If you want lots of regulation— sometimes down to the specific height you mow your grass— they're great. If you don't, you might want to look elsewhere.

I used to see this as a country where people who worked hard were rewarded materially, but as a reporter, I saw when it stopped working that way for everyone sometime in the 1980s. Taxes have multiplied; food prices continue to rise, and medicine is out of reach for many who need it every day.

So, what is causing it to be so hard for ordinary people while government officials have the best health care, pensions, housing, and opportunities?

As of September 2021, a Congressperson's annual starting salary was published as $174,000 to $193,000, with raises limited to 3-5 percent a year. But wages don't tell the whole story. Many benefits the average person does not get are also published at https://www.google.com/ search?q=what+is+a+cogresspersons+starting+salary&rlz=1C1GCEA_

Editorial comment: That's a long way from the $50 a year paid to those in Congress in 1789, which was the first year anyone received pay to represent the people. I know it's not near what the top CEOs of corporations get paid, but benefits (and connections) make up for that.

Is it an editorial comment to state that it looks as though things seem to be heading toward a two-tier America? There are enough examples of what I mean by that they could fill another whole book, so I'll just give just one example of what many communities have lost.

There is a tremendous physician shortage in poor communities, but the wealthy seem to have no trouble finding specialists and plastic surgeons. Why do so many physicians choose high-paying specialties over being an ER or rural doc? Are these doctors just selfish?

No!

Interviewing physicians, I've heard some say they start out studying to become general practitioners in low-income neighborhoods that need them most, often where they grew up. I've done news stories on this over the years, and most of the time, I have been told they had to choose a high-paying specialty because they came out of school carrying so much debt. Some still devote their lives to low-income communities, but then they're saddled with debt for years, and no student debt— can ever become part of a bankruptcy— should it get to be too much of a load to carry. According to Education Data.org https://educationdata.org/average-medical-school-debt the average medical school student leaves with $215,900 debt, over and above the educational debt for college education before attending medical school.

Some of us older people remember when the neighborhood Doc came to our homes, right into our bedrooms, when we were kids and had a fever or sore throat, arriving with their little black bags and medicines. Big pharmaceutical companies and insurance didn't dominate the industry then, just sixty years ago.

Dr. Ellenson and Dr. Goldstein, our doctors from Asbury Park, N.J. in the 1940s and 1950s, didn't ask what was *covered*. They just gave us shots, or bandaged our wounds, took some cash, and went back to their homes, where most had their offices in spare rooms. Sometimes, people didn't have the money to pay them, but that was usually worked out somehow.

Life in this country was different then. Notice I'm not saying "better for everybody" because of gains in opportunities for women and (not enough, but) less racial divide. *But it was different,* and so many of us who were grown and already set in homes and families and careers by the mid-1980s never saw "starting life" the way it is for young people now. Many my age and older think because of technology, kids growing up now have everything at their fingertips, and life is easier for them.

I feel fortunate to have been a journalist during these changing years and also to have raised a grandchild born in 1998. These things have kept me in touch with changes many people my age didn't get to see. I have reported on changes as they happened, including interviewing people who lost their homes. *I've even interviewed women who lost their children to State Services because they'd lost their homes.*

So, who is winning, and why? And why does knowledge of any of this depend upon which news source you are using?

Shouldn't news be news? Where is the extensive coverage of things that affect multitudes of people? Just a few months back, there were news reports of tens of thousands of migrants living under a bridge in Texas, and four days later, the story died. The migrants are gone. Some dispersed into the US, and others were sent back. End of story, unless you or your community was involved. But all our taxes are involved or will be, in some way, whether to help migrants assimilate or to pay law enforcement to keep them away.

Is news so unimportant now that ten to eleven commercials in a thirty-second segment are more significant than following up on something affecting so many people? Yes, last week, I counted eleven commercials from the start to finish of the thirty-minute news program, NBC Nightly News, on my local station. Yes, I still watch *NBC Nightly News* even though I know its anchor, Lester Holt, has a net worth is $35 million, and his salary is $10 million a year. I don't "necessarily disapprove" of someone because they have money. Go ahead. Hopefully, you've learned enough now to search for who pays that money!

Many broadcast stations are owned by the same major corporations that operate political PACs. Some reporters may not even know who's behind their paychecks, but they certainly don't want to stop getting them. So, for now, let's just examine how political PACs and wealth relate to news.

Owners of vast and profitable companies haven't just been throwing money at politicians willy-nilly; they know when they have something to gain by seeing someone elected who will do favors for their particular industries. On the other hand, politicians need to find the money for billion-dollar (media) advertising, which makes for good marriages between the wealthy companies and corporations and politicians from local levels through counties, and state and even national campaigns all the way to Washington.

"Marriages" of this kind make it possible for special interests to get what they want and leave the general public out in the cold. The more money donated; the more favors are given to the special few with the most to contribute. All we have to do to see that is to take a good look at the *Citizens United* and FEC decision that makes it possible for corporations to funnel money to help their particular donor or industry.

We only mentioned the FEC decision briefly earlier, so let's examine a better explanation of it. **Along with the earlier decision on Citizens United, this case put the final nail in the coffin of "fair and equitable" politics.**

Oh, Come' on, Editorial comment alert! See how easy it is to slip an editorial comment into facts? "Final nail in the coffin." Whose opinion do you think that is?

Since together, these two decisions made a huge difference in political giving by billionaires and corporations, the 2014 decision on the FEC deserves a bit more explanation here. The information following about this case comes from the Encyclopedia of Alabama found online at McCutcheon v. Federal Election Commission - Encyclopedia of Alabama[5].

In 2014, *McCutcheon v. Federal Election Commission* (FEC) went even further than *Citizens United* did in 2010. Considered another landmark case, the Supreme Court ruled that campaign donations can be viewed as a form of "free speech" protected by the First Amendment to the U.S. Constitution. The lawsuit challenged FEC restrictions on the *amount* of donations to candidates in federal elections and national political parties. The suit was filed by Jefferson County[6] Alabama resident Shaun McCutcheon and the Republican[7] National Committee because the regulations limited the number of candidates individuals could support, thereby denying donors their constitutional rights to free expression and free association.

"McCutcheon, the initial plaintiff in the case, is the founder and CEO of Coalmont Electrical Development, a mining-related engineering firm in McCalla, Jefferson County. A member of the Jefferson County Republican Party Executive Committee, McCutcheon has supported Republican candidates and the national party for many years and believed that his free expression rights and association were restricted by the two-year limits on political donations. At the time of the lawsuit, contributions to federal candidates and political parties were limited in two ways. One,

---

5.   http://www.encyclopediaofalabama.org/article/h-3895

6.   http://www.encyclopediaofalabama.org/article/h-1370

7.   http://www.encyclopediaofalabama.org/article/h-1500

contributors were capped at $2,600 per donation. Second, they were also limited to a total of $46,200 in combined contributions to federal candidates and $70,800 to federal political action committees[8] and national political parties in a given two-year period—McCutcheon's lawsuit aimed at the second restriction.

He argued that he should be able to donate the maximum amount to as many candidates as he wished but that the "aggregate restrictions" (combined restriction level) prevented him from doing so. As he noted in an interview in the newspaper *Politico,* he said he "saw no reason to believe that donating to 18 candidates rather than the capped 17 will increase corruption in the electoral process." He further argued that the limits favored incumbents, giving them an advantage over challengers.

As reported by the Associated Press, the Supreme Court made a stunning reversal to the nation's campaign finance laws when it ruled 5-4 on that case, saying that the premise of "free speech allowed large entities, including corporations and labor unions, to spend on political campaigns directly."

I'm sure all this makes more sense now than it did when "campaign donation laws" were first mentioned in previous chapters. Pages and pages of legalese came down to that one sentence (directly above).

Anyone who wants to read the entire document may see it at http://sers.fec.gov/fosers/showpdf.htm?docid=305685. This link opens to the Federal Register, October 21, 2014, from which this chapter was researched, along with the other sources mentioned.

The only other thing readers might want to know about following the money is what is known as "Dark Money," a term that comes up now and then about donations, especially in politics and news.

The definition of dark money given in online Webster's Dictionary is "funds raised to influence elections by nonprofit organizations that are not required to disclose the identities of their donors."

---

8.   http://www.encyclopediaofalabama.org/article/h-1490

One online definition goes on to explain why they call it dark, saying, "political spending by nonprofit organizations, for example—501, certain kinds of nontaxable, nonprofit groups—are not required to disclose their donors. That means these organizations can receive unlimited donations from corporations, individuals, and unions."

Since this happened during his Presidency, it's not opinion to quote President Obama as saying at the time, "The Supreme Court has given the green light to a new stampede of special interest money in politics."

* * *

Before we go on to another chapter, I'd like to give you the most recent list of who hides the most $ $$$ in offshore locations —and where those locations are—(including a list of dedicated reporters working to expose it). Just go to

https://www.icij.org/investigations/pandora-papers/. This is an investigative report released in October 2021 by The International Consortium of Investigative Journalists.

As explained in an Associated Press report, dated Sunday, Oct. 3, 2021, "A global investigation has revealed how the rich and powerful have [been] hiding their investments in mansions, exclusive beachfront property, yachts and other assets for the past quarter-century... The investigation, dubbed the Pandora Papers[9], was published late Sunday and involved 600 journalists from 150 media outlets in 117 countries."

"The investigation is based on a leak of confidential records of 14 offshore service providers[10] that give professional services to wealthy individuals and corporations seeking to incorporate shell companies,

---

9.   https://theflipside.us15.list-manage.com/track/
click?u=281c839c990f42b374467ae5f&id=10e0cdbd91&e=4fb81f5c72

10.   https://theflipside.us15.list-manage.com/track/
click?u=281c839c990f42b374467ae5f&id=801cf7a0ed&e=4fb81f5c72

trusts, foundations and other entities in low- or no-tax jurisdictions." **ICIJ**

I won't go into it further here because there is enough information in just this first report on these papers to fill another whole book, and also because I promised to stick to "older" examples so as not to worsen the divisions we now have in this country. There will be follow-ups by the same consortium of journalists on the Pandora Papers investigation, so anyone interested can sign up on that site to be notified of those by email.

Another thing that has recently come to light was the subject of a segment October 10, 2021, airing of the news show "60 Minutes." It's called "Deep Fakes." I wonder why it is not being reported somewhere almost daily? Far less important things are followed much more closely. Deep Fakes are videos and still photos that can digitally put any person's head on a body and make any words seem to come out of that image's mouth. So maybe you *think*you're listening to someone and really getting the words of an opposing view from who you think is on your screen.

Frightening? I think so.

Because "Following the Money" and "Finding Good News Sources" often go hand-in-hand, there will be more about checking out donors and seeking truth in news in the next chapter while pointing to various ways to separate "real news" from "fake news."

Unless, of course, you're seeing a "Deep Fake."

12

So, How Can I Find the Truth?

Learning to be Your Own Reporter (Links & Sites)

As a forty-year journalist and lifelong freelance writer, I enjoyed looking up the statistics and legal cases referenced in this book. Now I'm going to suggest some ways you can do that, and even some sites to seek out the truth.

Readers already have a treasure trove of links they can follow, which is why I think this book is better read online, although I am also providing a print copy. Hopefully, this chapter will help you search for the truth amid so many lies.

Yes, I said lies. Now, I hope each reader asks (his or herself) if that is an editorial comment, because this is a tricky one. With so many saying someone else's view is a lie, how do you know who to believe?

One thing to look for in any news source is whether it conforms to the standards of the Society of Professional Journalists' "Code of Ethics," which can be found at https://www.spj.org/ethicscode.asp. That will probably eliminate (my guess) about eighty percent of the news sources we're exposed to today. It speaks of "presenting all sides of issues," and "doing no harm," "being sensitive to someone who a story might harm," and "taking responsibility for accuracy and context" of what is printed under your name, and in the publication or station for whom you work.

Yes, about eighty percent. **(Please say that by now, you recognize my estimate as an Editorial Comment! Have I listed any data to back that up?)**

Is your print source a member of the National Press Club or the American Society of Newspaper Editors? They're both easy to check out online, as is the ownership of most American media.

Check out where their funding comes from too. That doesn't necessarily mean coverage will change, but it could if ownership has reason to want to influence the news. Start typing in things like "who funds" and put in your favorite news source. Then check out the top three or four donors in the lists that show up. It's amazing what you can find.

I certainly didn't know that Charles Koch was now involved with The Poynter Institute in St. Petersburg, Florida, until I wrote this book. It still looks like it is teaching journalism in the same honest manner as always. So, does it matter that Koch is known for financing political activities nationwide?

Wikipedia says, "Charles Koch funds and supports Libertarian organizations including the Cato Institute, which he co-founded with Edward H. Crane and Murray Rothbard in 1977." In another place online, I found the statement (as sourced and quoted in an earlier chapter), "Charles Koch supported his brother's candidacy for Vice President of the United States on the Libertarian Party ticket in 1980." I could not help looking up The Cato Institute, a "Libertarian think tank" that can be found at https://www.cato.org/about

This is not saying anything "bad" about Charles Koch or his family or foundation. I have stated three facts about him in this book: he helped found The Cato Institute. He recently acquired an interest in The Poynter Institute, and he has Libertarian political beliefs. I have not heard any journalists say there is a difference in Poynter. This is just to point out *how to follow ownership if* you see a change in reporting style. Or if you notice a continuously slanted or one-sided way of showing or writing about people and events, especially political ones. Or, maybe just to see who funds your favorite news source.

Like China.

What? China has stock in an American news source?

Yes, and that certainly surprised me.

In 2014, a Hong Kong-based investment group called Integrated Whale Media purchased[1] a majority stake, more than 310 shares, in *Forbes Media,* one of the United States' best-known media companies.*Forbes Magazine* is known worldwide for its annual lists. The magazine is renowned for its lists and rankings, including those of the wealthiest Americans *(the Forbes 400), America's Wealthiest Celebrities,* the world's top companies *(the Forbes Global 2000),* the Forbes list of *The World's Most Powerful People,* and *The World's Billionaires.*

Will China change how Forbes covers stories involving China and its allies like someone who came with new ownership changed my headline and first paragraph of two of my stories in Chapter 1? Nothing says it will, but I am trying to explain to readers that all is not what it seems, and there are good ways to check your news source right from your desk.

Remember in Chapter 1 how I said to be sure and check me out as your source first thing, before listening to anything I had to say? The same thing goes here. Check out every source before you believe what you read, hear or see.

There's a lot of information on national media on sites like *The American Journalism Review* or *The Columbia Journalism Review.*

Have there been any significant changes in your news sources lately? In an age of manipulated and polarized news, if you aren't willing to at least hear the arguments on all sides of issues, you can't even think about calling yourself a well-informed citizen.

Media companies are fighting to stay afloat in the face of the Internet, which has grabbed a large share of their advertising revenue through avenues like Google, Amazon, and the big tech companies. Book publishing has also been affected. Three of my former publishers have shut down, so the books I had with them are no longer in print.

---

1. https://www.nytimes.com/2015/11/06/business/dealbook/forbes-sues-integrated-whale-media-over-deal.html

Rainbow's End Publishing Company in Baden, Pa., published my first book *If I Should Die Before I Wake,* and sold it to colleges for women's studies in 1992. *America Star Books* closed a few years back, leaving another of my books in online limbo. In 2016 I self-published *The Sumerian Secret,* romantic suspense, and in early 2021, my nonfiction spiritual book, *True Stories of Help from the Other Side,* was published by *Sunbury Press Inc.,* Mechanicsburg, Pa.

When I'm working as a manuscript editor, I try and gear my clients toward solid companies because the truth is, they're getting harder to find in this economy. Tell-all political exposés seem to be coming out every day, and **THE INFORMATION YOUREAD IN THEM IS NOT NEWS**. They're books, and books come from the perspective of the author. Publishing companies choose whether to publish certain books, and readers choose which ones they want to buy.

That is nothing like news.

News choices should be based on truth, not what someone wants to read, hear or watch. Someone who watches television news or reads print publications that continually bash one "side" of an issue or political party and make gods out of the other side (or party members) are not giving you news. At best, they're giving you commentary, and at worst, propaganda. If you don't remember the difference, just look back at Chapter 5.

<u>**This is My List. I'll Bet Every Reader Has One in His or Her Head!**</u>

<u>**What Media Should Tell You What Most Media Tells You**</u>

What's going on in the world	What celebrities drive and wear
What's bad for us in our food	What diet celebrities are on
What's in our water supply	What celebrities eat & drink
What people are running from in S. America	No answer to border conditions
Why U.S. summers are hotter than ever before	Time to enjoy the sunny beach
Why winters are colder than ever before	Holiday decorations are up early
Who buys or sells major media	What politicians are (stupid/smart)
Five minutes every day on Congress's actions	What politicians are (stupid/smart)
The pros AND cons of gun ownership & reform	What is (stupid/smart) about guns
How major police depts. are looking into reform	*Defund* the police? (stupid/smart)
Ways groups are learning to work together	Racial hatred & bad behavior
How small businesses are/can survive tech buying	Amazon, Amazon, Amazon
What other nations are doing about climate change	Ignore or scare about changes
What innovations in solar & wind are taking place	Ignore/scare about fossil fuel jobs
Medical innovations & research	Insurance ads (5-8 each break)
What & why species are declining or moving	Ignore/ or scare (ex: killer hornets)
How some are helping/housing homeless	Ignore unless unavoidable (LA)
More Town Halls with Red & Blue together	Keep them separate (stupid/smart)

These are just a few observations. I'm sure each reader has their own list of things they think are more important than a lot of what they're hearing, reading, or seeing in their newscast.

Now I'm going to give a few easy-to-find (some free— some take small donations only and some just because so far, they check out as balancing their content).

I have thoroughly checked this first source and tried to find bias. Somewhere. Anywhere. But when I checked out each of its reporters, I found they had an equal number of conservatives reporting on the "conservative side" of every issue as they did "liberals" reporting on the "liberal side" of that same issue.

I checked their bios. I checked other things they had written online. This source has no idea I am mentioning it at this time, although I plan to send them a letter, and of course, a book when this is published. To their excellent job of "recapping" issues and then putting up a red box and a blue box with each ones' arguments, I say BRAVO, and believe me, I say that loudly. It's called *The Flip Side*. Just type it into any search bar and enjoy seeing both sides of each important issue. Or, to make it easier yet, just click here if you're reading this in an online format. https://www.theflipside.io/

Even readers who don't think the other side of an issue has any merit at all, seeing both sides of important issues side-by-side can give you a starting point to discuss things without arguing. Sure, you might never change your opinion, but wouldn't it be nice to know why family members and friends oppose what you say?

Besides *The Flip Side,* there's *1440 Media* at https://join1440.com/. I haven't found any bias there, but I haven't studied the background of those on its reporting staff yet like I did *The Flip Side*. Maybe some of you will want to do that yourselves. *1440 Media* says it scours a hundred news sites every day before publication. It's relatively new, but it appears exceptionally trustworthy so far, so try it out and see what you think.

The site with the longest history of truth and investigation into money in politics is at https://www.opensecrets.org/elections-overview/biggest-donors. The Center for Responsive Politics in Washington DC runs this site. This organization is said to be the nation's premier research and government transparency group tracking money in politics. Its main donors are the Sunlight Foundation, The Pew Charitable Trusts, the Carnegie Corporation of New York, Open Society Foundations, the Joyce Foundation, and the Ford Foundation.

At its site (link above), you can type in names and even election cycles, and a whole list of top billionaire donors, PACS, and corporations will pop up, in order, starting with the highest donor. Along with mountains of other information, Open Secrets lists individuals and corporations that gave political donations to political parties or individual campaigns and how much tax break they get by working the system. Legally, of course. **Nowhere in this book has anyone been accused of doing anything illegal. Besides helping**

people find information the way journalists do; it aims to inform citizens about rules that allow the wealthy class to avoid taxation legally.

Sheila Krumholz, longtime executive director of the Center for Responsive Politics, states on the site, "In our thirty-five years of following the money, we've never seen a court decision transform the campaign finance system as drastically as Citizens United. Now we have a decade of evidence, demonstrated by nearly one billion dark money dollars, that the Supreme Court got it wrong when they said political spending from independent groups would be coupled with necessary disclosure."

In 2019, Krumholz testified before the US House of Representatives Subcommittee on Improving Lobbyist Tracking Data. Near the end of her testimony, she is quoted in government records as saying, "We respectfully request the addition of unique identifiers for individual lobbyists that are currently available only internally to the offices of the Clerk of the House and Secretary of the Senate to the publicly available data files that are updated daily. If the addition of such identifiers is not possible at this time, we request that a study be undertaken to determine the feasibility of doing so in the future."

After reading the full report of her testimony, we can see that The Center for Responsive Politics understands that individuals can violate gift limits to individual politicians by using variations of their names, such as Jane Doe, J.A. Doe, J. Anne Doe, and Mrs. Robert Doe. The way government reporting is done, no distinction is made public to show if this is the same individual. The contents of Krumholz's testimony explains that well. It can be read in its entirety at https://docs.house.gov/meetings/AP/AP24/20190402/109212/HHRG-116-AP24-Wstate-KrumholzS-20190402.pdf.

* * *

Several random things I found on *Open Secrets* are worth mentioning. For instance, in 2020, the Pfizer Corporation and its affiliates gave $16 million to (a political party- I don't want to look biased by naming it, so just look it up yourself) and, by the way, Pfizer received a $39 billion dollar tax cut that same year.

GE and Chevron are the next top donors to political campaigns and also received billions in tax cuts after donating. Just look it up. The two takeaways I hope to give readers are recognizing editorial opinion (or worse, propaganda) and digging out the truth for yourself like seasoned reporters do.

I realize many people are too set in their opinion to care what others think, especially about religion and politics. Still, it never hurts to understand someone else's perspective, even if it's to find a good argument that counters it. Just be sure a "discussion of facts" is really not a discussion of some broadcaster's or podcaster's opinion.

That's why I chose to make all my Editorial Comments in Bold, like this quote: "Once people learn to separate truth from fiction, I believe the world will be a much better place for everyone."

Before we stop talking about good sources of straightforward news, I want to mention a few more: First, there's *Pulitzer Newspapers* found at www.Pulitzer.org[2]. The problem with this site however, is that it isn't a day-to-day source of breaking news, but reprints of the best and most factual stories its reporters find.

Another one I want to point out is *The Hill* that operates both print and television. Yes, it is owned by The Nexstar Media Group, the one that bought out Media General Inc., where I worked for Sunbelt Newspapers and had the headline and first graph of more than one story changed. But I have never worked at Nexstar and cannot pass judgment on how it is to work there. What I can say is that *The Hill* is distributed daily to all Congressional offices and has a lot of

---

2.   http://www.Pulitzer.org/

information on policy that can be read online at https://thehill.com/policy.

The reason I am naming this as a good source is because of three awards it has won from trustworthy media organizations. Back in 1997 it took The National Press Club's annual Sandy Hume Memorial Award in recognition of its reporting on an attempted Republican coup against then-speaker Newt Gingrich[3].

Then in 2019, *The Hill* won the Society of Professional Journalists' First Prize for Features with *Celebrities Dive into Midterms* and also for its series *How the Trump Tax Law Passed*. In 2020, it again won an award from the Society of Professional Journalists' —a First Prize for Features, for the story *Inside the Secret World of the CIA's Social Media Team*.

I also want to remind you here of the site I mentioned in Chapter 9: Harvard University's "Future of Media Project. I am going to be going back to that from time to time to see how it changes since they say they regularly update their lists. I'll repeat the link here so it's easy to find now, as you read this: https://projects.iq.harvard.edu/futureofmedia/US-media-index

I'm sure there are others. Readers have probably found a site or two that are writing or broadcasting non-biased news in various geographical areas, and if you let me know about them, I will be sure and feature them on my Blog, *Americans for Truth in News,* found on my website, which is listed with my other online coordinates in the back of this book.

* * *

As for how media changes have affected politics, I discussed Democrats and Republicans throughout this book because they are the two major parties here. Still, I want to mention that as of November 2020, there were 225 state-level ballot-qualified political party affiliates in the

---

3.   https://en.wikipedia.org/wiki/Newt_Gingrich

United States, with some parties recognized in multiple states. For example, both the Democrat and Republican parties are recognized in all fifty states and account for 102 of the 225-total state-level parties. Three minor parties were recognized in more than ten states as of November 2020 because of their numbers: The Green Party, The Libertarian Party, and The Constitution Party.

For more information on this and other ballot-related party information, just type in "list of registered political parties in the United States." Several were there as of August 2021, but the one that's easiest to read and seems most complete is https://en.wikipedia.org/wiki/List_of_political_parties_in_the_United_States

I put that in to show that government agencies can give you a lot of information. Some I have used to get statistics are "government housing," "veterans services," and other specific topics.

Another way to check whose money is behind the news stations you watch on television or the newspapers you read is to check out who their shareholders are. You can find out the names of the shareholders of a company (and CEOs and CFOs) using several resources. Suppose you want to find out the names of significant shareholders of a public company. They would be filed with the SEC (Securities & Exchange Commission). In that case, you can find this information by searching EDGAR, the SEC's Electronic Data Gathering, Analysis, and Retrieval System, at https://www.sec.gov/edgar/search/

To find most things, just type in words like "shareholders at MSNBC or CBS or CNN" or whatever you're curious about. I just type in what you're searching for right in the Google search bar, like "who funds Fox News," or who funds the weekly show, "60 Minutes."

For example, "who funds CNN" brings up a site that says, "It is owned by CNN Worldwide, a unit of the WarnerMedia News & Sports division of AT&T's WarnerMedia. In 1980, American media proprietors Ted Turner and Reese Schonfeld founded it as a 24-hour cable news channel. From there, you can look up Turner and

Schonfeld, and in this case, refer back to the chapter in which we talked about large media buying smaller ones. We covered Warner quite extensively there, but we did not get into "their beliefs," or "their slant," or anyone's here because that is not the purpose of this book. The goals here are to show you we are being spoon-fed many programs that pass as news and how you can distinguish fact from fiction.

The Internet is sucking up many of the major television stations' advertising revenue, and there is currently a lot of conjecture about who will end up in control of it. We should all watch for this in the future, as more and more people get their news from Internet sites.

How many of us have already been censored (or cyber-jailed or banned) from a social media platform for political posts?

EDITORIAL COMMENT: I fear this is only the beginning if control slips into the hands of any group intending to influence large numbers of citizens who are unaware of the ownership and policies behind the news stations they watch. The Internet has already proven to be filled with foreign bots and algorithms that "pretend" to be human.

As I was concluding my research for this book, I stumbled across a site that claims to have the bias of the different news sites scientifically "measured." Percentage of right-wing, percentage of left. You might want to take a look at this site, too, although I haven't checked the accuracy of its percentages because there doesn't seem to be any way of doing that without watching each channel a lot more than once.

Still, it might be a good thing to look at and see if any of it matches up with the things you find on *Open Secrets* or *The Flip Side* or *1440Media*or whatever else you choose to follow. But here it is if you want more help finding sites to start your digging: https://towardsdatascience.com/how-statistically-biased-is-our-news-f28f0fab3cb3. It's owned by Crunchbase, which, if you "follow the money far enough," you find is owned by Oracle Films, and the financers behind that are also available online. I didn't go any further with that one, but some of you might like to. There are some really interesting names on its first page.

Another print and online publication worth following appears to be *The Guardian* newspaper. Although The Guardian Media Group in London owns it, it has no shareholders and is operated by The Scott Trust. In 1936, the trust was named after its longtime editor CP Scott. A portion of the trust's purpose states that the paper is "to operate with no shareholders or billionaire owners, so it can set its own agenda and provide trustworthy journalism that is free of commercial and political influence."

More can be found at https://www.theguardian.com/gnm-archive/2014/dec/18/histories-of-the-newspapersfor those who want to study it further themselves. The Guardian has had ongoing reports from several correspondents in Ukraine since the start of the recent Ukraine-Russian war.

I hope that this book will teach readers how to search out the truth in today's "Wild West of News." Most of us know all news organizations report on events differently. Right now, the biggest concern is the Internet. There are arguments for and against regulation, just as there were with "The Fairness Doctrine," which used to regulate fairness to all sides of issues in print and broadcast. As we saw at the beginning of this book, it died because both Congress and the FCC skirted the key issue in their decisions concerning "free speech vs. media regulation." Without the Fairness Doctrine or something like it, anyone can say anything and swear it is true. That may be good for lawyers specializing in libel suits but not for the public.

Loss of The Fairness Doctrine combined with rules enlarging corporate news sources' coverage area means millions of people get news funded by just one source. This calls for each person to learn to be their own reporter. No one needs to tell any of us what can easily happen once all the dissenting voices are quashed. I lived in Germany in the 1960s as a military dependent and met many Germans who still had clear memories of what happened before and during the war.

So, lets' end with this Editorial Question: "Do you think money could now purchase an entire industry, including media, just like any other commodity, or will our elected representatives and founding documents and principles prevent that from happening here?" I feel all citizens must know exactly how (and where to go) to follow the money. That is why I have tried to teach readers how to be "their own reporters and seek out the truth."

* * *

Next Up by This Author:
CONFIDENTIAL CLIENTELE
A story of homelessness, addiction, redemption and love.
78,000 words. Fiction. Romantic-Suspense.
Pre Orders starting in July. Release date: December 26, 2022.

Other Books by This Author Found on Her Website
www.pennyfletcher.com [4]
THE SUMERIAN SECRET
Mystery and murder surround clay texts predating the Bible by thousands of years. Can a tenacious reporter uncover secrets in government vaults without being detected, and will the attentions of a NASA scientist and wealthy robed translator affect her quest?

The Atlantic Book Review

"The Sumerian Secret is an intense, emotional novel, well developed and appealing to a wide audience especially those who enjoy works by Steve Berry, Sydney Sheldon, and Danielle Steele. Lots of historical and science fiction, and romance, written with intelligence and wit. You will lose yourself in this story."

4.	http://www.pennyfletcher.com/

TRUE STORIES OF HELP THE OTHER SIDE

Published by Sunbury Press, Mechanicsburg, Pennsylvania

This memoir of Fletcher's life is written as an interaction with the Universe, signs of spiritual intervention, and an unshakable faith in God. From her orphanage beginnings and one brutal marriage, her faith, grit and fortitude allow her to find happiness both in marriage and highly-regarded in the profession she always desired.

About the Author:

A print journalist and editor for more than 38 years, Penny Fletcher has written more than 12,000 news stories, features, and editorials and earned more than 20 press awards from The Florida Press Association and Community Papers of Florida. As a reporter and Bureau Editor during several takeovers, she has seen and felt many of the changes she writes about in Dirty News first-hand. After leaving the newsroom, she made an in-depth study of the Supreme Court, Congressional, and FCC rulings that have led to the disinformation, commentary and biased reports passed off as news over the last 25-or-so years.

While working full-time as a journalist for 'Sunbelt Newspapers' and was a columnist for 'The Tampa Tribune,' on the side, she wrote for magazines as varied as 'Gulf Coast Fisherman,' 'Today's Christian Woman,' and 'True Story'. She also freelanced as an editor for Amazon's first publishing venture, BookSurge, where she transitioned from Associated Press to Chicago style in both American and British English, and still operates an editorial service on her website www.pennyfletcher.com where she has edited more than 250 books. Until 2021 she also gave once-a-week classes in creative fiction writing at The Center 4 Lifelong Learning in the nearby retirement community of Sun City Center.

She self-published a romantic suspense novel, 'The Sumerian Secret,' in 2016 and was traditionally published by Sunbury Press of Mechanicsburg, Pennsylvania, in 2021, in the spiritual genre, with 'True Stories of Help from the Other Side'.

A native of the Jersey Shore, during her first marriage, she lived in many states and in Europe as a military dependent, but has now resided in Florida for more than 40 years. The mother of four children and two "children from another mother," she also adopted and raised a grandchild who is now also grown. She says one of her most significant accomplishments is helping start two shelters for victims of domestic abuse, after having survived it herself, before meeting her late husband in 1981. Her first book was a first-person account of domestic abuse, 'If I Should Die Before I Wake'. It was published by the former Rainbow's End Publishing Company of Baden, Pennsylvania, in 1992, and is still available online in used copies.

She is currently press-credentialed by the Florida Freelance Writers/ Writers & Editors Network. Her blog, 'Americans for Truth in News,' is updated weekly on her website where she talks about history, current events, politics— and of course, news.

I really appreciate you reading my book! Here are my social media coordinates:

Smashwords Author Page: https://www.smashwords.com/profile/view/PennyFletcher

Friend me on Facebook: https://www.facebook.com/profile.php?id=1242871933

Follow me on Twitter: https://twitter.com/pennyfletcher

Favorite my Smashwords author page: https://www.smashwords.com.pennyfletcher/

My D2D Author page: https://books2read.com/ap/ngkBoG/Penny-Fletcher

Subscribe to my blog AMERICANS FOR TRUTH IN NEWS: https://pennyfletcher.com/penny-fletchers-blog/ [5]

Connect on LinkedIn: https://www.linkedin.com/in/penny-fletcher-a981388/

Visit my website: www.pennyfletcher.com [6]

• Sign up for my monthly newsletter: *Write Your Heart Out*

• Check out my editing & coaching experience, testimonials, and fees

---

5. https://pennyfletcher.com/penny-fletchers-blog/

6. http://www.pennyfletcher.com/